A MEDICAL SCHOOL IS BORN

by

Robert Straus

*A History of the Conception, Gestation
and Infancy of the University of
Kentucky College of Medicine
By One Who Assisted in the Delivery*

Cover design and book layout by James Asher Graphics
Photographs, used with permission by University of Kentucky and the
Lexington *Herald Leader*
Dust Jacket Photo by Ann Stroth

Manufactured in the United States of America

Publishing House
Kuttawa, Kentucky

All book order correspondence should be addressed to:

University of Kentucky, College of Medicine
Office of Development
Chandler Medical Center
800 Rose Street
Lexington, KY 40536-0084

CONTENTS

William R. Willard, M.D.
Founding Dean of the College of Medicine
(1956-1965)
and Vice President of the
        University of Kentucky for the Medical Center
(1956-1970)

DEDICATION

To William R. Willard. His vision, his leadership and his tireless effort left an indelible mark on the University of Kentucky College of Medicine and on student-centered medical education and patient-centered health care nationally.

ACKNOWLEDGEMENTS

The original suggestion for this book came from Emery A. Wilson, current Dean of the College of Medicine and a graduate of its class of 1968 who has also provided continuing encouragement and support. Others who read preliminary versions of the manuscript and provided valuable suggestions are Howard W. Bost, my colleague on the planning staff and later Assistant Vice President and then Vice Chancellor of the Medical Center; Frank G. Dickey, President of the University of Kentucky from 1956 until 1963 during the critical period of planning for and activation of the College; Peter P. Bosomworth, the College's first Chairman of Anesthesiology, Dr. Willard's successor in 1970 as Vice President for the Medical Center and later, until his retirement in 1994, Chancellor of the Medical Center; Robert L. Johnson; Arnold M. Ludwig; Rick Smoot; Kenneth Cherry; and Thomas F. Garrity. The title "A Medical School is Born" was suggested by an article that appeared in the *Journal of Kentucky Medical Association* in October, 1960.

During the preparation of this book I also had an opportunity to meet with many others who as colleagues, students or friends of the College experienced the College's early history and shared their memories with me. Special thanks for their time and their recollections are extended to William K. Knisely, George W. Schwert, Joseph B. Parker, John W. Greene Jr., Roy K. Jarecky, Harold D. Rosenbaum, John S. Sprague, Howard W. Beers, William R. Markesbery, William T. Maxson II, Jacqueline Noonan, and Edmund D. Pellegrino. My thanks also to Frank B. Stanger of the University of Kentucky Libraries for his help in locating archival materials.

In this endeavor, as throughout my career, Ruth Straus has been my most staunch supporter and most valuable critic.

PREFACE

The College of Medicine at the University of Kentucky admitted its first students in the fall of 1960 following four years of intensive planning and development. It became the 86th medical school in the United States and one of the first of more than 40 new medical schools that have been developed since World War II.

Prior to the 20th century, medical education in the United States had been haphazard at best with few standards and a great range in the nature and quality of the educational experience. This situation changed dramatically following the 1910 Flexner Report on Medical Education in the United States and Canada that was based on a study commissioned by the Carnegie Foundation for the Advancement of Teaching. The influence of the Flexner Report in bringing about the reform of medical education and establishing standardized criteria for accreditation was so powerful that, by the 1930s, the requirements and curricula of the nation's medical schools had become virtually identical. Following World War II, many leaders in medical education were expressing concern that medical schools were not keeping pace with important changes in the knowledge and technology of medicine, in the health problems and expectations of the population, or in knowledge about the educational process. Yet, proposals for experimentation and change in medical education, such as a boldly different curriculum that was introduced at Western Reserve University, tended to be shot down before they could be tried out. Although many leaders in medical education recognized the need for and were publicly advocating reform, those forces that favored maintaining the status quo had successfully resisted change in nearly all existing institutions.

The development of a completely new medical school at the University of Kentucky provided a rare opportunity for those who were concerned about stagnation in medical education. This was an opportunity to start from scratch without a faculty who felt most comfortable doing what they had always done, without facilities that resisted renovation, and without traditions and regulations that were set in concrete. This was also an opportunity to develop programs that would be specifically designed to meet the needs of the College's constituents; its students, its patients and the people of Kentucky.

When Dr. Emery A. Wilson, Dean of the College of Medicine, invited me to prepare a history of the early development of the College, I accepted this opportunity with pleasure for several reasons.

First, I was one of four planning staff members who came to Lexington in September 1956 with Dr. William R. Willard, the College's first Dean (and Vice President of the University for the Medical Center) to help develop the College of Medicine and the Medical Center of which it was to be a part. I stayed on, filling several roles in the College until my formal retirement in 1987, and remain actively involved as an emeritus professor. Thus, my identification with the College runs deep.

Second, I experienced first hand the challenges and the rewards of developing a new medical school literally from the ground up. We started with a corn field, and were unencumbered by traditions, existing buildings, inflexible personnel or ideological preconceptions. We were given time to study the unique needs and expectations of Kentucky, to develop a set of philosophical objectives, and to select architectural features and initial personnel that were compatible with these objectives. We visited a majority of the then existing medical schools in the United States asking colleagues what they would do differently if they had our opportunity to "start from scratch." When its doors opened in 1960, the University of Kentucky College of Medicine began with an innovative and bold curriculum; a set of objectives that were focused on the needs of students, patients and the people of Kentucky; and a physical plant that reflected these objectives in ways that were both functional and unique.

Third, I have experienced the entire history of the College.

I have known and tried to help resolve many of the problems and challenges it faced as the events of the last forty years have brought changes in society, higher education, the economics and politics of health care delivery, and the sciences and technologies of medicine; changes that were undreamed of in the 1950s.

Finally, I welcome the task of recounting and interpreting a history that I have personally lived. The definition of history is much broader than a mere chronology of events. It includes an interpretation of their causes, sequences and consequences. In this history of the development of the University of Kentucky College of Medicine, I shall try to be objective, though necessarily selective. However, I hope that readers will appreciate that I have been far too involved personally in the experience of these events to avoid some subjectivity in their interpretation.

Medical education in Kentucky has a long history. This history along with a review of events and personalities that were prominent in paving the way for a College of Medicine in Lexington will be reviewed briefly in Chapter One.

In 1956, the Kentucky Legislature, following the recommendation of Governor A. B. Chandler, appropriated an initial five million dollars toward the establishment of the Medical Center at the University of Kentucky. The first step taken was to conduct a national search for an individual who could provide leadership and direction for this development. This search resulted in the recruitment of Dr. William R. Willard, a man who was to become recognized as one of the outstanding medical educators and statesmen in the United States in the 20th century. Chapter Two will provide a profile of Bill Willard and attempt to show how his earlier career reflected the philosophy, convictions and leadership qualities that would mold the College of Medicine through the years of planning and initial activation.

One of Dr. Willard's conditions before accepting the position at Kentucky was that he be given adequate time and resources for planning. He wanted to study the existing conditions and social needs of Kentucky; consult nationally with the best minds concerning desirable directions for medical education; prepare a set of objectives that would reflect both needs and forward thinking in medical education nationally and factors that were of special importance in Kentucky; develop positive relationships and incorporate the best thinking of key individuals representing the University, State government, the medical and other health professions and community leaders; and develop a clear statement of philosophy of medical education as a basis for architectural design, faculty recruitment, curriculum development, selection of students and the design of patient care programs.

Chapter Three will describe some aspects of the setting in 1956 - the University, the Lexington community, the State and its government - in which the development of the College of Medicine and Medical Center would begin to take place. It will also consider the rationale for the planning process and identify the initial planning staff.

The first task of planning was the development of a statement of philosophy of medical education for the University of Kentucky. Because this statement, as it was prepared and refined in the fall of 1956, provided both guidance and a rationale for much of the College's development, it is reproduced as Chapter Four of this history. Chapter Five will describe the planning process, covering the period from the fall of 1956 to the fall of 1960 when the first students arrived.

Planning led to implementation. Chapter Six will cover the years of initial activation of the College beginning in September 1960 when the first class matriculated and extending to the late 1960s. By then, Dr. Willard had relinquished the role of Dean (remaining as Vice President for the Medical Center) and the College of Medicine was developing its own administration and identity as distinguished from those of the Medical Center.

By 1970, events totally unanticipated in the planning process were imposing major changes on the organization, structure, and financing of medical education and medical care. Chapter Seven will consider how the College of Medicine adapted through three decades of rapid change when many of the invations that characterized its early years gave way to the pressuresof unanticipated events, needs, and demands. By 1990, some of the concerns about medical care and the education of physicians that prompted Kentucky's innovations of the 1960s had come full circle. The fresh perspectives of a new generation of faculty and leadership have led to a revitalization of many of the College's originally unique objectives for curriculum, patient care and community responsibility that were ahead of their time in 1960. Once again Kentucky is a recognized leader in medical education innovation.

Some of the history of the College of Medicine is insepa rable from that of the Medical Center. This is especially true of the events that led up to the establishment of the College and the Center, and of the years of planning (1956-1960) and early activation (1960-1966) before the offices of Dean of the College and Vice President for the Medical Center were separated. The other colleges of the Medical Center - Nursing, Dentistry, Allied Health and Pharmacy - each have had a distinct history of their own. Other major units of the Medical Center - the Medical Library, the University Hospital and the Kentucky Clinic - will be considered primarily as they relate to medical education. Although some consideration is given to the entire 40-year history of the College of Medicine, the primary focus, as the title suggests, is on its periods of conception (Chapter 1 and 2), gestation (Chapter 3 thru 5), and on its birth and infancy (Chapter 6).

Chapter One

THE ROOTS RUN DEEP
Medical Education in Kentucky in Historical Perspective

In the perspective of history, the College of Medicine is a relatively "late-comer." Its forty year lifespan represents only a fifth of the two centuries for which there are records of medical education in Kentucky. The earliest such records are found in late 18th century references to fees paid by apprentices to practicing physicians, many of whom were themselves apprentice-trained.

Formal medical education was first provided in Kentucky by Transylvania University which created a medical department in 1799. Thus, just 34 years after America's first medical school had been established in Philadelphia, Transylvania joined the ranks of Pennsylvania, Harvard, Columbia and Dartmouth as one of the country's few universities to offer medical education and the first such endeavor west of the Allegheny mountains.

Two professors were appointed; one in chemistry, anatomy and surgery and the other in materia medica, midwifery, and the practice of physic. Students apparently took courses when they could find time and afford the fees. No degrees were awarded during the first 18 years of the school's history. However, Transylvania's first professor of chemistry, anatomy and surgery, Dr. George Brown, began in 1799 the collection of books that has become Transylvania's historically valuable medical library.

Transylvania's medical school was put on a firmer footing in 1817 with the appointment of five new faculty and the enrollment of 20 students. However, the school was apparently a victim of internal strife among its faculty for its entire history. Charles Caldwell, who came from Pennsylvania in 1819 as the school's first Dean, wrote in his autobiography "I had under my direction, one of the most miserable Faculties of medicine . . . that the . . . human family can well furnish, or the human mind easily imagine." Although enrollment increased to as many as 281 students in the 1825-26 year, the school continued to suffer from faculty rivalry and factionalism. In 1837, following a general economic decline in Lexington that was exacerbated by a cholera epidemic, a majority of the faculty left to teach at the Louisville Medical Institute that had been established in 1833. The Transylvania trustees temporarily dissolved the faculty of medicine in 1837. When the school was revived a short time later, there was continuing instability of its faculty and declining enrollment of students. By 1850 there were only 92 students. For several years the faculty split their time teaching a fall term at a newly established Kentucky School of Medicine in LaGrange and a spring term at Transylvania. Finally, in 1859, Transylvania graduated its last six medical students and the school was closed. There was a brief effort on the part of former medical faculty to revive the school in 1874 but this was discontinued four years later. (John H. Ellis, *Medicine in Kentucky*, Lexington, University Press of Kentucky, 1977.)

It is perhaps a commentary on the sad state of American medical education generally in the 19th century that Dr. William H. Welch, one of the founders of the Johns Hopkins School of Medicine, is reported to have said "of all the early medical schools, we have come to believe that Transylvania was the best." (Quoted in Kentucky Medical Foundation, "The Urgent Need: Kentucky Must Have More Doctors," Lexington, 1955.)

Scattered records indicate that as many as 15 medical schools existed in Kentucky for some period of time during the last half of the 19th century. Most of these were undersupported and short lived. During this period the primary locus of medical education in the State was in Louisville.

In 1846, the Louisville Medical Institute became the Medical Department of a newly formed University of Louisville. Rivalry between the University's Medical Department and the Kentucky School of Medicine became bitter and intense. A third school, the Louisville Medical College, opened in 1870 and a fourth, the Hospital College of Medicine, in 1874. In the late 1880s, the Louisville National Medical College was established to provide a medical education for blacks. This was followed in 1892 by the Southwestern Homeopathic Medical College. By the late 1890s there were between 1,200 and 1,500 students enrolled annually in Louisville's seven medical schools. Initially these had offered one year or less of instruction. However, with the establishment of the Association of American Medical Colleges in 1889, the creation of the National Conference of State Medical Examining and Licensing Boards in 1891, and a Kentucky Medical Practice Act of 1893 that gave licensing authority to the Kentucky State Board of Health, standards for medical education were established and the courses of study were extended at first to three, and then to four years by the end of the century. Still, goals and standards for accepting students, establishing curricula, and evaluating competence were minimal, reflecting the sorry state of medical education throughout the country.

In 1908, responding to increasing concern expressed by representatives of the educational and medical professions, the Carnegie Foundation for the Advancement of Teaching commissioned a national study of the status of medical education in the United States and Canada. This study was conducted by Abraham Flexner, an educator who happened to be a native of Louisville and onetime Louisville high school teacher. Flexner's Report on Medical Education led to the establishment of standards for medical education, many of which are still in force today and serve as a basis for the accreditation of medical schools.

By the time of Flexner's visit in 1909, only three of Louisville's medical schools came under his scrutiny, the University of Louisville having recently absorbed four of its rivals. Two of these he dismissed briefly. The Southwestern Homeopathic Medical College which had an attendance of just 13 students Flexner found "without merit. Its graduates deserve no recognition whatsoever, for it lacks the most elementary teaching facilities." Of the Louisville National Medical College with its 40 students, Flexner noted that students were accepted with less than a high school education and that the laboratory facilities were nominal, but that it was connected with a scrupulously clean hospital of 8 beds.

Most of Flexner's comments on medical education in Kentucky were reserved for the University of Louisville and these were scathing indeed. He noted "a large, scattered plant, unequal to the strain which numbers put upon it." He cited "radical defects for which there is no cure in sight. The classes are unmanageably huge; the laboratories overcrowded and undermanned; clinical facilities, meager at best, broken into bits in order to be distributed among the aggregated faculty. To carry the school at all, a large attendance is necessary; but a large attendance implies a low standard. The situation is practically deadlocked." Flexner found examples of students admitted from two-year high schools or less, without either the required examination or certificate and "in flat disregard of its professed standard and of the state board." (p.34) Instruction at Louisville and elsewhere was primarily by didactic teaching and "by quiz-masters who drill hundreds of students in memorizing minute details which they would be unable to recognize if the objects were before them." (p.84) The hospital facilities he noted were "poor in respect to both quality and extent: unequal to the fair teaching of an even smaller body of students, they are made to suffice for the largest school in the country." (p. 229) Flexner found potential support lacking at both the financial and academic levels. Of the parent institution he said "we have indeed progressed too far in our social and educational development to use the word 'university' for an enterprise of this kind." (p. 231)

Flexner also took note of the University of Kentucky. He cited several other states where a merger of medical education into the state universities was logical and desirable. He then added "but in Kentucky, the state university is totally unequal to the task." He mentioned the State University's "educational ineptitude" and added "having now chosen a politician, without educational qualification or experience as its president, its immediate future promises little." (p.231) [Abraham Flexner. *Medical Education in the United States and Canada*. A Report to the Carnegie Foundation for the Advancement of Teaching. New York: The Carnegie Foundation, 1910.]

By 1912 all medical schools in Kentucky except the University of Louisville's had closed their doors. Fortunately, Flexner's criticisms of Louisville's medical school provided an impetus for changes that transformed that program into an accreditable institution. A municipally supported institution, the University of Louisville struggled continuously for adequate financial resources. However, during the years following the Flexner Report, it was able to assemble and maintain a qualified and respectable faculty, meet the national accreditation standards that were established, and become a significant provider of physicians for Kentucky. In 1948, in response to efforts by a group of University of Louisville medical alumni, and circumventing a provision of the Constitution that prohibited making appropriations to private institutions, the General Assembly created a Medical Research Commission that could contract with the University of Louisville Medical School. An initial appropriation of $125,000 per year that was increased by subsequent legislatures was a significant factor in keeping Louisville's medical school solvent until the University of Louisville became a state institution in 1970.

Abraham Flexner was not the first person to think of the logic of providing medical education at Kentucky's State University. There had been suggestions that the University's forerunner, known as the Kentucky State Agricultural and Mechanical College, should provide medical education. Then, in 1908, when the name of the college was changed to State University, the General Assembly specified that there should be introduced courses of instruction leading to degrees in both medicine and law. Although no extra funds were appropriated for this purpose, a College of Law was established in 1908. However, according to historian Carl Cone "Medical instruction was another matter. The president and trustees approached it gingerly and, after study, did nothing." (Carl B. Cone, *The University of Kentucky. A Pictorial History*, Lexington: University Press of Kentucky, 1989, p. 51.)

It was at about this time that Flexner reported that the intellectual climate of Kentucky's State University was totally unsuited for medical education. Flexner was wrong, however, in his estimate of the qualifications of the University's new President. Although he was not an academic scholar and his presidency was controversial, Henry Stites Barker saw the academic stature of the University substantially enhanced during his 8 year term of office.

In 1917, the school in Lexington was renamed University of Kentucky and the idea of a medical school was revived again by its newly inaugurated President, Frank L. McVey. McVey envisioned a medical center as an essential component of a great university but, as in the past, funds were not available.

A glimmer of hope that private resources might become available to build a medical school for the University occurred in 1928 when William Monroe Wright, who had prospered as founder and developer of the Calumet Baking Powder Company, retired to a horse farm in Lexington. Both Wright and his wife expressed some interest in contributing to the establishment of a medical college but the stock market crash intervened. Wright was later said to have regretted that the University did not have the $10,000,000 that he had lost in the crash and to have promised that if the market recovered he would build a medical center. However, within a few months the depression was in full swing and Wright was dead.

McVey's interest and vision did not lag and in 1928 he assigned Dr. John S. Chambers, newly named director of the University's Department of Public Health and Hygiene and of the Student Health Service, and his associate Harry R. Lynn to conduct a study of the availability of physicians and medical services in Kentucky and of their capacity to meet the needs for health care.

The report of the Chambers and Lynn study (*Medical Services in Kentucky*, Lexington: Department of Hygiene and Public Health, University of Kentucky, Volume 1, Number 1, January, 1931, 69 pp.) provided a thorough analysis of the supply of physicians and other health resources in Kentucky and of the distribution of these throughout the State. Although, in raw numbers, the supply of physicians was within prevailing national standards, they found serious problems of distribution, with most rural areas seriously deprived. Equally serious, they found that a majority of the then active practicing physicians were 50 years of age or older and had received their medical training in one of the "old system" medical schools that had existed before modern standards for medical education had been introduced. In keeping with the age distribution, they found that the ratio of physicians to population for the state as a whole was dropping rapidly with the rural areas being the largest losers. They concluded that Kentucky needed to offset its loses by adding at least 100 new recruits to medical practice a year; a goal that could only be met through an expansion of facilities for medical education within the state "either by adding to old schools or creating new ones." (p. 50) In addition to providing a thorough analysis, the Chambers and Lynn document was noteworthy for several far-sighted suggestions including the concept of consolidated health facilities and services in rural areas (following the model of consolidated rural schools), their emphasis on the need for training Kentucky's doctors to understand the culture and special health needs of Kentucky's population, and their reference to general practitioners, not as physicians with a minimum of training who are unable to specialize, but as "specialists in doing well many of the commoner things." (p.6) Dr. Chambers, commonly known as Brick because of his bright red hair, became a leading advocate for the establishment of a medical school at the University of Kentucky. Working within the Fayette County and State Medical Associations, he succeeded in attracting the interest and enlisting the support of prominent and vigorous physicians who eventually played an important role in bringing this about.

Concern over the inadequacy of medical resources in Kentucky continued to mount during the depression and war years. Following World War II this became the subject of numerous newspaper editorials and of discussions within the General Assembly. In 1948, a joint resolution was introduced in the General Assembly calling on the Board of Trustees of the University of Kentucky to study these needs and estimate the costs of establishing a College of Medicine "with accreditable standards and facilities." However, no action was taken at that time.

Three years later, in 1951, a group of Lexington physicians including Drs. Francis Massie, Edward Ray and Coleman Johnston appeared before the Board of Trustees of the Kentucky Medical Association to present the case for a State supported medical school at the University of Kentucky and seek the support of the Association. Opposition was strong among the Trustees, many of whom were Louisville graduates who feared a loss of existing State support for the Louisville school and a weakening of the school through competition.

Swayed by Dr. Massie's assertion that competition would strengthen Louisville and by support for the Lexington project from Dr. Sam Overstreet of Louisville, then President of the State Medical Association, the Trustees agreed to invite the Council on Medical Education and Hospitals of the American Medical Association to conduct a study of the need for a second medical school in Kentucky.

This invitation led to what is known as the Anderson-Manlove Report on Medical Education in Kentucky based on a visit to the State on April 17 and 18, 1951, by Drs. Donald G. Anderson and Francis R. Manlove of the AMA's Council. After meeting with Dr. Overstreet, Dean J. Murray Kinsman of the University of Louisville School of Medicine, the State Commissioner of Health, several other officials of the University of Louisville, the Mayor of Louisville and President Herman L. Donovan from the University of Kentucky, Anderson and Manlove concluded that as of 1951 Kentucky faced a serious shortage and maldistribution of physicians and was falling quite short of producing its share of the nation's physicians. They found a clear need for an expanded capacity for medical education in Kentucky. After reviewing the resources of both the University of Louisville and the University of Kentucky, and the supporting health and medical facilities and resources of the Louisville and Lexington communities, Anderson and Manlove concluded: "It would also appear that the most desirable way of achieving this expansion would be to establish a second medical school at the University of Kentucky in Lexington, and that in general the opportunity for developing a satisfactory medical school in Lexington would appear to be favorable." Although this report may have done little to assuage those who favored expanding support for the Louisville school or feared for its survival, it appears to have made a powerful impression on leaders within the medical profession and served as well to arouse renewed interest in medical education at the University of Kentucky. At about the same time a detailed "Memorandum on Medical Education in Kentucky," dated April 29, 1951, was prepared by Dean Kinsman of Louisville and Dr. Chambers of the University of Kentucky for the Council of the Kentucky State Medical Association. This document was noteworthy in that Dean Kinsman indicated that he would support the creation of a new Medical School at the University of Kentucky unless it meant withdrawal of adequate state support for the University of Louisville's school.

In response to the Anderson-Manlove recommendations, the Board of Trustees of the University of Kentucky issued a report on medical education dated February, 1952. Entitled "More Doctors for Kentucky" and probably prepared by Dr. Chambers, this report reviewed in detail a number of relevant documents including the joint resolution of the 1948 General Assembly regarding a College of Medicine at the University of Kentucky; the findings and recommendations of the Anderson-Manlove Report; and a forthright statement from Dean Kinsman of the University of Louisville, indicating that his school was not in a position to meet all of the State's needs. The report also contained much relevant data on Kentucky's supply and distribution of physicians, on the status of medical education in other states, and on the limited opportunities for Kentuckians who seek a medical education. It recommended that the General Assembly recognize the need for a second state supported medical school, endorse the concept of establishing such a school at the University of Kentucky, and seek from the Legislative Research Commission a study of all factors involved. The report emphasized that such an undertaking would be costly and must be supported without draining support from other responsibilities of the University.

In response to the Anderson-Manlove and the University of Kentucky Trustee's recommendations, the 1952 General Assembly passed a resolution directing the Legislative Research Commission to make "a careful and impartial study of the desirability and steps necessary for the establishment of a State-supported medical school at the University of Kentucky." In keeping with the Commission's policy of not making direct recommendations to the General Assembly, an Advisory Committee on Medical Education was appointed to work with the Commission and formulate recommendations from its findings. The members of the Advisory Committee were five prominent physicians, each from a different area of the State and each an alumnus of a different medical school. The Director of the Legislative Research Commission also asked President Donovan to appoint a University Committee to study the pros and cons of medical education from the perspective of the University of Kentucky.

The medical school committee appointed by President Donovan on November 20, 1952 included eight of the University's most distinguished faculty. After consulting with several nationally recognized leaders in medical education and gathering a mass of data, they delivered a report that was emphatically in support of the creating of a medical school at the University of Kentucky. They spelled out the implications in terms of graduate programs in the medical sciences, programs of postgraduate and continuing education for physicians, and the need to have educational programs for nurses, dentists, medical technicians and a close relationship with the existing College of Pharmacy. They spoke of a university hospital, a medical library and they provided fairly reasonable estimates of the costs for construction and operation. As an indication of their perceptiveness, they rejected a claim that Dr. Chambers had made when, in trying to show that the medical facilities in Lexington could support medical education, he included several thousand "beds" that were in psychiatric facilities. Instead, this group noted that Lexington was "sadly short of (general) hospital beds" as an added argument in support of the need for University Hospital. In this, and several other reports that were prepared at about the same time, it was pointed out that despite the existence of numerous medical schools in nearby states, very few students from Kentucky were accepted for out-of-state admission. Taking a lead from Dr. Chambers, the Committee emphasized that the development of a school to the point of graduating physicians would take many years and noted that even if early action were taken to initiate the process, it would be about 1965 before the first product could be realized. This committee of distinguished faculty members also were quite positive in noting that the addition of a medical school could only strengthen the quality of education and the stature of the University and place it in a position to seek greater State support for all of its programs. ("Medical Education at the University of Kentucky: A Report Prepared by the Medical School Committee of the University of Kentucky, for the Legislative Research Commission," 1953.)

The Legislative Research Commission's Report entitled "Medical Education: Does Kentucky Need a State-Supported Medical School?" was issued in November, 1953. (Legislative Research Commission, Research Publication No. 37.) It included the recommendations of the Advisory Committee on Medical Education. Drawing on the findings of previous studies the L.R.C. report addressed the question of need by examining the supply and distributions of physicians and other health personnel throughout the state. It examined the qualifications and age distribution of practicing physicians and compared Kentucky with other states. It also assembled data on where Kentucky residents were receiving a medical education and where Kentucky's current practicing physicians had gone to medical school. It then considered how a new medical school might be expected to increase

Kentucky's supply of physicians and how it might also be expected to address the severe shortage of physicians in rural areas. The Report included a thorough analysis of the costs that could be anticipated for building and operating a medical school in Lexington and the kinds of facilities that would be needed. It also addressed and rejected possible alternatives to creating a State-supported medical school as ways of meeting Kentucky's needs.

In presenting its findings and recommendations, the Advisory Committee praised the University of Louisville's School of Medicine for furnishing such a large share of the State's physicians and contributing to the medical welfare of the people of Kentucky. Its findings included: 1) a definite over-all shortage of physicians and other health personnel and a critical shortage in rural areas; 2) inadequate teaching and training facilities to satisfy the needs of qualified resident youth for medical education; 3) inadequate opportunities for interns, residents and other postgraduate medical training; 4) a limited ability of the University of Louisville's school to expand its capacity; 5) an overdependence of Kentucky on other states for the medical training of its citizens with future such opportunities to be curtailed by restrictions placed by other states on accepting out-of-state residents; 6) inequities in prevailing practices of charging patients who can afford health care to pay for the care of those who cannot; and 7) the Commonwealth has a responsibility in the interests of the public's health to provide its own citizens with educational opportunities in the health professions.

As a long range response to its findings the Committee recommended "that a School of Medicine be established in Lexington as a part of the University of Kentucky as soon as the Commonwealth's finances permit and assure the construction of an approved 'Grade A' medical school." As essential elements of such a school, the Committee recommended the construction of a teaching hospital with a minimum of 500 beds, a medical sciences building to accommodate classes that would graduate 75 doctors per year, adequate residence halls, the assurance of adequate financial support and the assurance of obtaining a competent dean and faculty. They also suggested that the Governor appoint a committee to study the problem of indigent medical care as it would relate to eligibility for admission to the University Hospital.

Responding to the Legislative Research Commission's Report and the recommendations of the Advisory Committee, as well as other evidence of need that had been accumulating over the past several years, the Board of Trustees of the University of Kentucky took formal action on June l, 1954 creating a College of Medicine to be activated at such time as adequate funding would become available.

Further support for a medical school in Lexington was building within the local medical professionals and business communities of Lexington and the entire Eastern portion of the State. In 1954, the Kentucky Medical Foundation was established as a non-profit voluntary organization dedicated to promoting the development of a medical school through public education and "grass roots" financial support. The Foundation was headed by J. Stephen Watkins, an engineer and member of the University's Board of Trustees. Its officers and trustees included more than thirty of the most prominent physicians, dentists, business executives and civic leaders in the area.

One of the Foundation's early actions was to reprint for wide distribution a paper on Medical Education in Kentucky by Dr. Brick Chambers, dated December 15, 1953. In this report, Dr. Chambers added to the findings and recommendations of his earlier studies, the argument that Lexington was already a major medical as well as cultural and educational center and was an ideal location for a new medical school on all three counts. He also advocated a position, supported by the Foundation, that the University and State must aim for quality by selecting the best possible person as Dean and then keep "hands off" and leave him free to select the "most distinguished faculty possible."

The Kentucky Medical Foundation became a potent political force in support of creating a new medical school at the University of Kentucky. Their influence was particularly important because of the opposition that was mounted by powerful forces that favored adding State support to expand the University of Louisville school. These included President Davidson of the University of Louisville, many of its prominent medical and other alumni, the Bingham family who owned the Louisville *Courier-Journal* and *Louisville Times*, and other politically powerful forces in the Louisville business community.

In 1955, the Foundation hired Russell E. White, who had been Comptroller of Transylvania College, to become its Managing Director. Under White, informational materials were developed for dissemination throughout the State; speakers were made available to medical, business, and civic groups; and endorsements were solicited from a wide variety of influential groups. These included county medical societies, hospital councils, teachers' associations, veteran's groups, farm bureaus, and civic service clubs. The Foundation's officers and members also were active in lobbying members of the General Assembly hitting away at the theme of one of their more elaborate publications - "The Urgent Need: Kentucky Must Have More Doctors."

In 1952, Albert B. Chandler, former Governor of Kentucky (1935-1939), United States Senator and Commissioner of Baseball, indicated his support for a medical school at the University of Kentucky. This became a key platform issue during his successful campaign for a second term as Governor in 1955. Shortly after assuming office, Chandler recommended to and obtained from the General Assembly an appropriation of $5,000,000 to initiate the development of a University of Kentucky Medical Center. On May 23, 1956, the University Trustees authorized the establishment of a Medical Center to include colleges of medicine, dentistry and nursing, a student health service, a medical library, and a University hospital. The Trustees, who were chaired by Governor Chandler, also initiated a search for an outstanding medical educator to provide leadership and direction for this undertaking.

Chapter Two

"AND I WOULD HAVE
NO OTHER"

Once an initial appropriation
had been made toward the construction of a Medical Center, the
first step of the University of Kentucky Board of Trustees was to
initiate a nation-wide search for an outstanding medical educator
to provide leadership for planning, development, and implementation. Direction for the search was entrusted to President
Herman L. Donovan who, because his retirement was imminent,
shared the task with his designated successor, Frank G. Dickey.
They were aided by a screening committee of about 35 faculty
members, university administrators and physicians from the community.

The search was to be guided in part by the special needs
of Kentucky that had been identified over the years and by a commitment of all concerned to develop programs which would meet
these needs with a degree of quality that would bring credit and
respect to the University and the Commonwealth. With Dr.
Vernon Lippard, Dean of the Yale University School of Medicine
and a nationally respected medical statesman as a consultant, the
committee first identified the role and the responsibilities of the

job and characteristics to look for in potential candidates. With suggestions from numerous leaders in medical education, a list of desirable candidates was assembled. According to Governor Chandler who, as Chairman of the Board of Trustees, was personally involved in the search, they were looking for "the best man in the country," the name of William R. Willard kept "coming forth," and, said Governor Chandler, "I would have no other." This view has been echoed by the then incoming University President, Frank Dickey, who remembers that four "outstanding candidates" were seriously considered but that, once he had met with Bill Willard, he was sure that they had found their man.

Dr. Willard brought to the University of Kentucky a unique combination of experiences, philosophy, personal style and commitments all of which were to leave their mark on the College of Medicine and the Medical Center. His impact on the College in its formative years was so significant that the history of the College cannot fully be appreciated without a review of the background of Bill Willard, the man.

In 1972 (the year he retired from Kentucky), Dr. Willard was selected by the Association of American Medical Colleges as recipient of the Abraham Flexner Award, its highest honor. He was selected in recognition of his "extraordinary contributions to medical schools and to the medical education community as a whole." In nominating him for the award, one of his colleagues called him "one of the great deans of all time." Another said that "the fruits of his labors are beyond reckoning, extending throughout the length and breadth of medicine." Another noted: "His sensitivity to the social, academic and political realities of our times is almost unparalleled." Still another wrote "when the annals of medical education for the second half of the twentieth century are written, it will require at least a chapter to delineate the significant contributions of William R. Willard."

In order to appreciate why President Dickey, Governor Chandler and other members of the search committee at Kentucky in 1956 were so convinced that they had found their man, this chapter will review some highlights in Bill Willard's earlier career. It will be seen that there were both compatibility and a continuum between Willard's earlier experiences and responsibilities and the values that he espoused and the requirements of the task in Kentucky for which he was selected.

Dr. Willard was born in Seattle, Washington in 1908. He attended public schools there and in 1927 was among a very small number of public high school graduates in the entire country who were admitted to Yale University. In order to attend Yale, he frequently had to hitchhike his way across the country to New Haven, and throughout his undergraduate years he supported himself by working on a job provided by the University and also as an independent entrepreneur, selling door to door to his classmates in their dormitories. He was graduated from Yale College in 1931, and, by combining his senior year with the first year of medical school he earned the M.D. degree from Yale in 1934. After an internship at Johns Hopkins and a residency in pediatrics at the University of Rochester, Bill Willard returned to Yale where he earned a doctorate in Public Health in 1937. Following several years as a Deputy State Health Officer in Maryland, Bill became an officer in the United States Public Health Service during World War II. In 1945 and 1946 he was assigned to direct the Department of Public Health and Welfare for the United States Army Military Government in Korea.

After completing his military service in 1946, Dr. Willard returned to Yale as an Assistant Professor of Public Health. There, he earned promotions with a rapidity that was most unusual at a school like Yale, becoming an Associate Professor in 1948 and a Professor in 1951. In addition, in 1948 he was appointed Assistant Dean of the Yale Medical School for Graduate Medical Education, and in 1949 he was selected by Connecticut's Governor, Chester Bowles, to be Chair of the Governor's Commission on Health Resources. While on the Yale faculty, Dr. Willard provided leadership for the development of continuing educational programs for physicians throughout the State and region. This was a new concept for Yale at that time and winning the cooperation and participation of Yale's medical faculty required great sensitivity, tact and a power of persuasion. Willard also participated in or directed numerous studies of community health needs and resources and was a strong advocate of a university's responsibility to provide services and support for communities and the society-at-large. In his own teaching, he expanded the concept of public health to a consideration of social, cultural and economic factors that are significant to the causes, course, distribution and resolution of health problems. According to Dr. Ira Hiscock, Chairman of the Department of Public Health who had invited Willard to return to Yale and proposed him for his successive promotions, Hiscock fully expected that Willard would succeed him as departmental Chairman. (Personal communication, Ira Hiscock to Robert Straus, April 5, 1972.)

As Chairman of the Connecticut Governor's Commission on Health Resources, Willard initiated studies designed to identify unmet health needs and develop recommendations for equalizing access to quality health care for the entire population. Included were a study that identified a need for and recommended the establishment of a State supported medical school at the University of Connecticut and a study of existing programs of health insurance that addressed many of the same issues that are still unresolved today. The Connecticut medical school need assessment study in 1950 considered many of the same issues that were identified by the Kentucky Legislative Research Commission in 1953.

In 1951, the State University of New York (SUNY) assumed responsibility for the medical school of Syracuse University. At that time this was a financially burdened institution with a primarily part-time clinical faculty. The school was renamed by SUNY as its Upstate Medical Center, a national search was conducted for a new Dean and William R. Willard was selected.

There were numerous challenges facing Bill Willard when he went to Syracuse. One was easing the transition of the medical school's faculty and staff from Syracuse University to the State University of New York. As might be expected some loyalties ran deep and there was much concern about becoming part of a large multicampus, state-supported bureaucracy. There was also a need to cultivate trust and mutual support with the administration and faculty of Syracuse University, an immediate geographic neighbor, where some people resented the intrusion and takeover of "their" medical school by the state institution, and a law suit was pending to resolve differences between the two university administrations. A second task was to transform a college of medicine with the single primary goal of training medical students and house officers into a regional medical education center with broader functions extending out into the community and the larger surrounding area. There was also a need to recruit a new faculty in many areas, especially for the clinical departments. Under Syracuse University, the school had drawn most of its clinical faculty from the practicing physicians of the community, many of whom devoted a limited number of hours a week to medical education. Plans for the State University called for developing a full time faculty for each of the clinical departments. In many instances this would require displacing physicians from their valued and prestigious academic positions while trying to retain their good will and loyalty. The new Dean was also faced with the task of designing substantially expanded and modern classroom and laboratory facilities for the basic sciences, recruiting some new faculty in these areas, and avoiding the hostility and suspicion of current faculty while motivating them to engage in needed curriculum updating and revision. There was a need to prepare for the design and construction of a new University Hospital. Through all of this there was a need to develop trust and mutually supporting relationships with the health professionals of the area, and with representatives of the business community and the city, county and state governments. Also crucial to the role of the Dean was the ability to interpret to representatives of the central SUNY administration and state government the resources that would be needed to achieve all of these goals, and to win their approval and support.

Six years later, when Dr. Willard left Syracuse for Kentucky, he had either accomplished or achieved significant progress on most of these tasks. He had turned bitter court actions between SUNY and Syracuse University into a spirit of conciliation. At the time a Syracuse University official characterized Willard as "remarkably capable of making others understand the point of view he is presenting." (Syracuse *Herald-Journal*, 7/29/56.)

By involving members of the local medical society in decisions regarding the development and staffing of full-time clinical departments, and opening the door for those physicians who wanted to be considered for full-time faculty appointments, Willard was able to win the trust and support of the medical community. By working closely with community and regional hospital councils and helping in their formulation of plans for new building programs and mergers, he was able to win the admiration of many who feared and fought the competitive impact of a new University Hospital. Working with local and state public health and welfare officials he helped to enhance the role of the medical school in providing health services for the indigent. In the words of one hospital official "You have to admire him... The way he can get in a meeting and adroitly bring together conflicting opinions is nothing short of magnificent." (Syracuse *Herald-Journal*, 7/29/51.)

One of Dr. Willard's major innovations in Syracuse was in the area of medical school curriculum and was based on a basic philosophical conviction he later brought to Lexington. As he had demonstrated in his years at Yale and his role with the Connecticut Health Resources Committee, Dr. Willard was a firm believer that health care is a social phenomenon and health status is governed by social, cultural and other behavioral as well as biological factors. He was convinced that the education of future doctors should include the social and behavioral sciences. Therefore, one of his early acts at Syracuse was to create the first position for a social scientist in a United States medical school that was fully supported by the basic budget and in a tenure track. He also persuaded the faculty of the College to provide three hours a week during the entire first year of the curriculum for a course in the social and behavioral sciences. He advocated teaching an emphasis on disease prevention as well as diagnosis and treatment and an emphasis on health of the family as well as the individual. He recruited as Chairs of the Departments of Psychiatry, Pediatrics, and Public Health men who shared this perspective and commitment. He appointed to senior faculty positions a health economist, a health educator, and a medical social worker, all of whom added new dimensions to the learning experiences of medical students and represented new dimensions in medical education at that time. He extended the impact of the medical center by providing continuing medical education programs for health practitioners of the entire north central area of New York State, and provided need assessments, consultation and collaboration for numerous health departments and agencies in the area.

Although construction on new facilities for teaching and laboratories was well underway in 1956, the steps leading to ground breaking had taken five years and Dr. Willard had been stymied in his efforts to obtain approval for a new University Hospital from the local medical and hospital leadership who feared competition, and from the bureaucratic labyrinths of the SUNY central administration and the New York State government. When he mentioned this frustration while he was being recruited by Kentucky, Governor Chandler promised him that if he came to Lexington, a University Hospital would be up and operating before New York State made "a hole in the ground." On this matter, Governor Chandler proved to be a prophet.

Much of Dr. Willard's effectiveness during his six years at SUNY's Upstate Medical Center in Syracuse, and at Yale before that, was related to his personal attributes and his style of leadership. From the time when I first met him, in New Haven in 1949, I was attracted not only by his philosophy, intellectual depth, and values but by my realization that he was a man of innate goodness, absolute integrity and total commitment to the responsibilities that he assumed. Because he drove himself without mercy, he inspired those who worked with him to exert extra effort as well. Long before joining him in Syracuse and accompanying him to Lexington, I had become accustomed to work sessions that might not end till 11 pm, or might start at that hour and go on through the rest of the night. Although he delegated tasks cleanly, he remained intellectually involved, raising appropriate questions and providing supportive suggestions. He was generous with praise for work well done. When less than pleased, he was impersonal, gentle and constructive with his criticism. Like Harry Truman, he assumed responsibility when problems arose. He believed in the democratic process, seeking, listening carefully to, and usually following the considered advice of those who worked with him. However, he reserved for himself the prerogative for making final decisions and did not hesitate to exert the authority that was appropriate to this ultimate responsibility. From people who he recruited, I have heard over and over again that their primary reason for accepting his offer of a job was the attraction of an opportunity to work with Bill Willard. This was certainly a major factor in my own moves from Yale to the State University of New York at Syracuse and from there to the University of Kentucky.

Hopefully, this brief review of Dr. Willard's career before he was appointed to lead the development of a new College of Medicine and Medical Center at the University of Kentucky, will help to explain why, when Kentucky was engaged in the search process, the name of William R. Willard "kept coming forth" as "the best man in the country." In many respects, Kentucky provided Bill Willard with an opportunity to bring a philosophy and a set of personal values and commitments to a setting where compatible needs and objectives had been defined, where his particular style of leadership and administration would be accepted and supported, and where there would be fewer barriers of resistance to change and a fertile field for innovation. At the same time, Kentucky found in Bill Willard a man with an established record as an innovator, who had already demonstrated an interest and success in addressing many of the basic issues that were identified by the Legislative Research Commission and the several other groups that had studied Kentucky's needs and recommended the establishment of a medical school at the University of Kentucky.

POSTSCRIPT

In 1972, the year that Bill Willard retired from the University of Kentucky, Frank G. Dickey, by then the Executive

Director of the National Commission on Accrediting, paid tribute to Dr. Willard in a letter he wrote to Dr. John A. D. Cooper, President of the Association of American Medical Colleges. Dr. Dickey wrote:

"Dr. Willard, in his quiet but most effective way, has contributed immeasurably to the medical education field and to the better understanding of the place of health programs in our larger society. He is a man of tremendous ability; his sensitivity to the social, academic, and political realities of our times is almost unparalleled.

"During the period that I served as President of the University of Kentucky, the Medical Center of that institution grew and developed. The one man responsible for its success and for the contributions it has made and continues to make is Bill Willard.

"The contributions of Dr. Willard, however, go far beyond the mere development of a school and a health center. His ability to understand and enunciate in a most effective manner the social and political problems in the health field have made him stand out as a real leader. He has proven that a truly service oriented program can produce solutions to many of the problems that have been confronting our educational programs for several decades.

"Above all, however, he is a man of integrity, unselfishness, and rare judgment. He was able to develop an outstanding program in a state with really limited resources. He accomplished this 'miracle' in a period when financial resources were not as plentiful from any of the usual sources as they have been in more recent years. He was willing to undertake this developmental task ... at considerable risk to an already established reputation in the field of medical education. But the major point to keep in mind at all times is that he not only succeeded, but produced results far beyond the expectations of those of us who were interested in and concerned about this program." (Letter of April 7, 1992 from Frank G. Dickey to John A. D. Cooper.)

In 1979, seven years after he retired from Kentucky, Dr. Willard was honored for his work in establishing still another pioneer program in medical education at the University of Alabama in Tuscaloosa. At this program, Julius B. Richmond, then serving as the Assistant Secretary for Health and Surgeon General of the United States, paid tribute to Bill Willard's special contributions. Speaking of the time that he had been recruited by Dr. Willard to become Chairman of Pediatrics at SUNY Syracuse, Dr. Richmond said: "Bill Willard entered my life at that time—1953—and he challenged me to embark on something that I could see only in outline on the far horizons of my career. But I could not resist. Like so many others, I also gambled on the vision of this unique teacher. None of us who gambled can say we lost. ... From the moment we joined him, we were to be the gainers, and through him ... the community would be the winner."

Turning to Dr. Willard's role at Kentucky, Richmond continued "I would have to mark Bill's work in Kentucky as a truly pioneering enterprise, one which would change the course of medical education and health services in our country. There was no pre-existing institutional history and tradition to overcome in Lexington. Like other pioneers in his native West, Bill Willard was challenged by new ground and plowed his own unique furrow in the wide open fields. ... He developed the concept and the physical institution of the health sciences center integrated into the life of the surrounding community. I would suggest that Bill's accomplishment was a prototype of the kind of institution that has come along and flourished in our Nation during the past decade. Bill did it first and ... there are many who would suggest that it has not yet been done better. ... The field that Bill was plowing was not part of the landscape of mainstream medicine 23 years ago. Many of his colleagues preferred to drive by and not notice his lonely work. But how we envy his crop!" (Julius B. Richmond, "Some Thoughts on a Quiet Pioneer," Remarks to honor Dr. William R. Willard, Tuscaloosa, Alabama, October 25, 1979.)

Chapter Three

THE SETTING

My initial association with the University of Kentucky College of Medicine began on the evening of June 3, 1956 in the living room of my home in Syracuse, New York. I remember the date because it was my wife Ruth's birthday and she was sick in bed when Bill Willard dropped by for a chat. This night, rather than discussing one of our Syracuse projects, Bill told of his being invited to review plans for a completely new university medical center in Lexington, Kentucky. He ruminated about his six years at Syracuse, what he felt had been accomplished and what remained to be done. Then he said that he had been invited to direct the development in Kentucky. He was obviously attracted to the challenge and the opportunity, but hesitant because all of his goals for the Upstate Medical Center had not yet been realized and because he felt a sense of responsibility to those, like me, whom he had brought to Syracuse. With a lump in my throat, I assured him that he had no obligation to me. He then said that, if he decided to go to Lexington, he hoped that I would go with him. This brought on another lump as I thought of the implications of a move.

We had first known Dr. Willard in New Haven. I had worked with him on several studies for the Connecticut Governor's Commission on Health Resources. After he moved from Yale to become Dean of the State University of New York's Upstate Medical Center, he invited me to join him there and to establish a program of social science teaching and research. Things had gone well in Syracuse both professionally and for our family. The social science program now included three other faculty, our fourth child was born there, and we had been living for about nine months in our "dream house" that Ruth had helped design and in which our family was thriving. In a brief moment I thought of our exciting teaching program, of the research that was in progress, of the many good friends we and our children had in Syracuse, of the impact of another move on my dear wife, of giving up our brand new house and neighborhood — and yet, I believe I knew then that if Bill Willard decided to go to Kentucky, we would be going too. True to her spirit, Ruth sensed the excitement of the opportunity, swallowed her disappointment at being uprooted so quickly, and gave the move her full support.

Despite my strong inclination to accompany Dr. Willard to Lexington, I withheld a decision until I could go to Lexington to see and be seen. Having grown up in Connecticut and never lived in the "South" I had some regional prejudices and I wondered if I had any right moving my wife and small children there. In particular, I worried about the quality of education and the values to which our children would be exposed. Lexington could not have had a better salesperson than Frank G. Dickey, newly installed President of the University who met my train at the old Southern Railroad depot on Broadway. Frank, who had previously served as Dean of the College of Education, was just the authority I needed to suggest that public education in Lexington might be superior to that of Syracuse (he was quite right) and to review the strengths and weaknesses of the city and county systems and suggest neighborhoods where the best schools could be found. Frank, a "southern gentleman" if there ever was one, also convinced me that southern society could be accepting of aliens from the north and that the University he headed genuinely hoped that we would come. Supporting Frank were several members of the Sociology Department, who with their distinguished chair Howard W. Beers, could not have been more kind and welcoming to an outsider who was being thrust into their midst. Several of these sociologists and their wives have been among Ruth's and my close friends for forty years. The clincher was a sign hung across Main Street near the Lafayette Hotel that announced "Big Top Peanut Butter - Made in Lexington". Our six year old daughter Peggy lived on peanut butter, not any ordinary peanut butter; it had to be Big Top. I phoned Ruth and told her it was "o.k." - we could make the move.

Events at the University of Kentucky moved quickly in the spring of 1956. After the State Legislature approved Governor Chandler's request for an initial appropriation of five million dollars, the University Board of Trustees lost no time in officially establishing a Medical Center on May 28th. Anticipating this action, the University administration had engaged appropriate consultation and proceeded to define the responsibilities of the position of Vice President of the University for the Medical Center and Dean of the College of Medicine. A screening committee that included faculty, administrators and representatives of the practicing medical profession had already identified and recommended candidates for the position. University President Herman L. Donovan, supported by his designated successor Frank Dickey and Governor Chandler, then lost no time in offering the position to Dr. William R. Willard. By July 19, 1956, Dr. Willard had accepted and his appointment had been approved by the University's Board of Trustees.

In negotiating the terms of his appointment, Dr. Willard requested authorization for a planning group and support staff who would assist him in the three year (later extended to four year) process of bringing the Center to the point of activation. Beginning with the formulation of a basic philosophy of medical education, the planning process was to include working closely with architects to assure that the facilities to be constructed would be functional for their intended use. It involved seeking a collaborative rather than confrontational relationship with the

University of Louisville where the University President, many alumni and the local press and power structure had vigorously opposed the establishment of what they perceived as a "competing," state supported medical school. It involved working closely with the leaders of the health professions in Lexington and statewide to keep them informed, seek their input and encourage their continuing support. It involved initiating studies of the health status and needs of the people of Kentucky, of the nature and distribution of existing resources, and of prevailing health beliefs, attitudes and practices of different segments of Kentucky's population. It involved reviewing the current status of medical education in the United States and identifying areas where change and innovation were particularly needed. It involved working closely with the faculty and administration of the University of Kentucky, trying to ease the apprehensions of those who feared a negative impact of the Medical Center on the rest of the University, and building on the support of those who would foster a close relationship between medical center and general campus goals and programs. It involved establishing criteria for the admission of students and the development of a curriculum, a program for patient care and an administrative structure. It involved the recruitment of key faculty to head the various departments, each of whom in turn would themselves recruit others. It involved working closely with both the State and Federal governments to interpret the needs for adequate funding for construction of the necessary teaching, research and clinical facilities and adequate operating budgets as well. To our planning group, it seemed as though all of these issues needed attention at once. All were interrelated. For example, many architectural questions depended on decisions regarding curriculum and patient care.

Because of the time required to design and build needed facilities, architects had already been designated when Dr. Willard was selected. Recognizing that the local architects lacked experience in the design of such specialized facilities as a medical science building and a hospital, the State agreed to employ the services of a consulting architectural firm, Ellerby and Company, who were specialists in the design of medical facilities. Ellerby had recently completed work on the design of a new Medical Center for the University of Florida and new facilities for the Mayo Clinic and they brought a particularly relevant level of expertise and experience to the task in Kentucky. The process of planning, design, requesting bids, and awarding a contract for construction imposed a tight time table that was further intensified by the time required to prepare and process applications to the Federal Government for the construction grants that were then available for both health research facilities and hospitals.

A FACILITATING FACTOR

Bill Willard had experienced some significant problems in Syracuse with respect to his relationship to the parent State University of New York and the state government. As the Dean of the State University of New York's Upstate Medical Center, Willard was three steps removed from the decision making process regarding both capital expenditures and operating budgets. He and his counterpart from the Downstate Medical Center reported to an Executive Dean for Medical Education in Albany, who in turn reported to the SUNY central administration and trustees, who in turn negotiated with the Governor, the Legislature and various officers of the central state government. This had required an incredible amount of time and energy in travel and negotiation. It often resulted in serious distortions in or modifications of communications as they were filtered through the multilayered process.

When he was being urged to come to Kentucky, Bill Willard had decided that he would consider a move only if he could have a more direct line of communication with those who would make ultimate decisions regarding both financial and academic matters. In Kentucky at that time, all state financed construction projects were the responsibility of the Department of Finance. Thus, the 5 million dollar appropriation for the Medical Center went to the Department of Finance, not the University. It was agreed that the Medical Center as the designated "user" would work directly with the State Department of Finance regarding relationships with architects and contractors. Since no funds were designated to pay for the planning process, a portion of the original appropriation was deposited by the Department of Finance with President Dickey for processing outside of the University's budget. Later the Medical Center personnel would be actively involved in interpreting, justifying and negotiating an operating budget that would be a separate request, additive to and not competing with the overall University budget. Although the arrangement was to be nullified in 1964 at the insistence of President Dickey's successor, Jack Oswald, it proved to be a critically important factor in facilitating the complex process of planning for, creating and activating both the College of Medicine and the Medical Center.

THE PLANNERS

According to Frank Dickey one of the many factors that convinced him that Bill Willard was "the man for the job" was his concept for a planning staff. Of the four individuals that Dr. Willard proposed bringing with him to Lexington, just one was a physician; the others were an economist, a statistician and a sociologist. This was in keeping with Bill Willard's perception of the tasks to be done and his conviction that medicine was a major social and economic institution and that the practice of medicine does and medical education should involve the social as well as the biological sciences. Of special significance also was Dr. Willard's determination to design the Medical Center to meet the needs of its constituents. This would require developing a broad base of information about the population to be served. He envisioned as part of the planning process gathering data on health status, needs and beliefs; patterns of response to health problems; the nature and distribution of existing heath resources; and factors affecting access to and utilization of health care including economic and educational status, and means of transportation and communication. Because the Medical Center would eventually involve a significant number of students, faculty and other employees, he envisioned that another function of the planning process would be to project the impact of these additional people on the University, the Lexington community, and the region.

The physician, Richardson K. Noback, had received his medical training at Cornell University and New York City's Bellevue Hospital. A specialist in internal medicine, he had been selected to direct the Syracuse Dispensary, an outpatient program for indigent patients that served as a teaching resource for the medical school.

The economist, Howard L. Bost, was originally recruited by Dr. Willard to come to Syracuse from the University of Michigan where he had earned the first Ph.D. degree in Health Economics to be awarded by an American university. His experience included working on health related matters for Walter Reuther of the United Auto Workers and work with the Commission on Financing Hospital Care. In Syracuse he was involved in a number of studies pertaining to the economics of health care delivery and regional health planning.

The statistician, Alan Ross, had most recently been a research associate in biostatistics at the University of Pittsburgh School of Public Health, while completing his Ph.D. at the University of Iowa. Because of his interest and capability in applying statistics to problem solving, he was initially recruited by Bost to work with him at Syracuse, but before he could move his family, he was invited to become a member of the planning staff at Lexington instead.

The sociologist was Robert Straus. I had received my Ph.D. at Yale in 1947. My dissertation, a study of historical and social factors associated with the assumption of responsibility for health care by governments, predated the development of formal graduate programs in medical sociology. I then served on the Yale faculty of Applied Physiology for six years, working in the field of alcohol studies. Also while at Yale, in addition to working with Dr. Willard's Governor's Commission on Health Resources, I directed the planning for a new State agency to provide residential treatment for emotionally disturbed children. In 1953, I joined Willard in Syracuse with the opportunity to develop a program of social and behavioral science teaching and research.

The appointments of Bost, Noback, Ross and Straus at

Kentucky were effective September 1, 1956. A fifth member to join the planning staff in January 1957 was Richard Wittrup, administrator designate for the University Hospital. Wittrup brought with him six years of experience in the University of Chicago Clinics that included responsibility for administering the Argonne Cancer Research Hospital and serving as assistant director of the University of Chicago's Graduate Program in Hospital Administration.

For Bost, Noback and Straus, planning for the University of Kentucky's Medical College and Center began in August in the living room of the Willard family home in Syracuse. There, in a series of late night sessions, the essence of what became the formal statement of "Philosophy of Medical Education for the University of Kentucky" was first developed.

Because the development and recruitment for Kentucky had moved so quickly all of the new appointees were faced with obligations to fulfill standing commitments at the same time that there was an urgent need to be involved in Lexington. For me, this meant two months of commuting by train in order to meet a teaching obligation in Syracuse while beginning to work in Lexington and another two months of sharing a small student apartment in Cooperstown with Noback and Willard while our families were selling homes and preparing for the move to Lexington. As would be the case with our planning staff roles, we each assumed different responsibilities; Willard did the laundry, Noback the dishes and dusting, and Straus was the cook (with long distance telephone instructions from Ruth).

THE SETTING - COMMUNITY

In the fall of 1956 when the planning for the College of Medicine commenced, the University of Kentucky, the Lexington community and the Commonwealth of Kentucky were very different than they are today. The State's population was approximately 3,000,000. Of these, about half a million were living in the Louisville-Jefferson County metropolitan area, and about 100,000 in Lexington and the other areas of Fayette County. Two thirds of the population lived in small towns or rural areas. There were no Interstate highways and only three short stretches of four lane divided highway in the entire state. Large areas of rural Kentucky were still without paved roads and even paved highways tended to be narrow and hazardous. The 90 mile trip from Lexington to Cincinnati could easily take three hours and twice that on weekends when families from Eastern and Southern Kentucky tended to travel home to their roots.

Lexington was a community with two governments; one for the incorporated city and one for the rest of the county. As a result of piecemeal annexation there were virtual islands of city surrounded by county and islands of county surrounded by city. The larger community was supporting two school systems, two police and two fire departments and two court systems as well as two "central" governments. At that time, Lexington still had a vibrant downtown with four department stores and a concentration of retail trade that was rivaled only by some shops in Chevy Chase and along the recently opened Southland Drive.

Horse farms and tobacco farming, for which the area was best known, surrounded the city in all directions. City streets turned into rural roads beginning at about Southland drive on Nicholasville Road, Lane Allen on Harrodsburg Road, Mason Headley Road on Versailles Road, at the newly developed Meadowthorpe subdivision on the Leestown Road, beyond the recently completed "beltline" from Georgetown Road to Winchester Road and beyond the Idlehour subdivision on Richmond Road. Local transportation was provided by an aging fleet of small busses. Residential telephone "service" was primitive with newcomers required to wait several months and then receive just a four-party line.

In the early 1950's, however, a long standing policy against the encouragement of any kind of industrial development had given way to the solicitation of "clean" industry. Such firms as General Electric (light bulbs), Square D (electrical equipment), and Dixie Cup (paper products) had come to Lexington and they were followed in 1956 by IBM that planned to employ as many as 6,000 people in the manufacture of electric typewriters.

The largest category of employment in Lexington was "medicine." In 1956, Lexington was said to have the highest concentration of specialty board certified physicians per population of any city in the country. For many years Lexington had served as a center of medical care for a third of the State's population. One recently opened (Central Baptist) and two long standing (Good Samaritan and Saint Joseph) general hospitals provided almost 900 beds. In addition there were a Shriners Hospital for crippled children, the Cardinal Hill Hospital that had been established to treat victims of polio, a soon to be closed T.B. hospital, and all together about 4,700 psychiatric beds in the State supported Eastern State Hospital, a Veterans Administration hospital and a hospital for narcotic addicts run by the United States Public Health Service.

Public transportation in and out of Lexington was shared by two intercity bus lines, two railroads and three airlines. Frequent bus service connected Lexington with most other cities and towns of the State and major terminals in Cincinnati and Louisville. The Southern Railroad provided its "Royal Palm" and two other passenger trains in each direction on a North-South route and the Chesapeake and Ohio Railroad still ran its "George Washington" between Louisville and Washington D.C. and New York City. Just four miles from the center of the city, Blue Grass Field was already served by Eastern, Delta and Piedmont airlines and was rapidly outgrowing its capacity for handling planes larger than the DC-3 for which it was designed.

Of Lexington's 100,000 people in 1956, the majority were from old Lexington families or Kentuckians who had migrated to the city. Although the black population of Kentucky was under 8 per cent, blacks comprised about 14 per cent of Lexington's population, a majority of them long time residents. Like much of America, race relations in Lexington were in transition. The railroad stations and bus station still maintained separate facilities, the air terminal did not. Hospitals were partially desegregated. Some theaters had segregated seating, others did not. In the older sections of town where a majority of the blacks lived, their homes were apt to be along the back alleys of white residential streets.

Outsiders were still a distinct and conspicuous minority in Lexington in the mid-1950's. To some of the old Lexingtonians these "new people" represented an unwelcome threat to their stable and valued way of life. However, the community's formal leadership and members of its power structure had decided to stake their future on growth, albeit growth that they intended to control.

For the medical center the planning staff there was a need to win confidence and earn acceptance and support in four distinct and critical areas; the community, the university, the state and among health professionals. Each of these were important and they all demanded attention at once.

Initially, Dr. Willard and his staff were inundated with invitations to receptions and other welcoming social events. Although designed by their hosts as expressions of hospitality, some of the other guests at these events expressed their ambivalence and even their regret about too much growth and the impact that all of these "outsiders" were going to have on the community.

Although I had never set foot in Kentucky before August 1956, it so happens that my father's family migrated to Kentucky in the 1840s. He was born and grew up in Louisville before going to college at Yale and eventually settling in New Haven. I quickly discovered that if I could find a way to mention my Kentucky ancestry, it would be assumed that I was "one of us" (and, therefore, should obviously also be concerned about too many "outsiders.")

THE SETTING - THE UNIVERSITY

Within the University of Kentucky, conflicting views and ambivalence about the impact of a medical center had existed since the possibility was first seriously proposed by President McVey in 1917. Following publication of the first Chambers study in 1931 and continuing to and beyond the establishment of the medical center by the Trustees in 1956, there were faculty and administrators who saw this as an opportunity to raise the support for and stature of the University to a new level, and others who feared that the Medical Center would drain already scant resources from the rest of the University and doom it to perpetual mediocrity. There were good reasons for concern. Only a few years earlier, the state constitution had mandated a ceiling of $5,000 for salaries of state employees including university personnel, and a successor ceiling of $12,000 had only recently been eliminated. In fact, in order to permit a salary of $20,000 for the new Vice President and medical Dean, the salary of the President was raised substantially to $21,000. The modest level at which the University was forced to operate was reflected in almost every area of expense. Few faculty members had private offices. Many departments had only one telephone line and only one secretary. In the entire University there was only one electric typewriter (in the President's office). One of my first assignments in Lexington was to prepare a memorandum that would justify on the grounds of economy and efficiency the purchase of additional electric typewriters.

With salaries that were far below the national average for comparable positions, faculty members bought most of their own supplies, and typed their own notes, manuscripts or correspondence on their own typewriters. Some laboratories were obsolete and some buildings were worn out. Benefits were minimal and the only provisions for retirement were through an unfunded plan that further drained the University's resources.

Recognizing the limitations within which the University was operating, those of us who came from the outside quickly developed an appreciation and admiration for the quality of education that was being offered and the level of dedication of many personnel at all levels. We welcomed the friendship of those who hoped we would help raise the standards by which the whole University was operating and we tried to understand the hostility or apprehension of those who assumed that we would further drain their already inadequate resources. Despite its limited resources, the University of Kentucky had achieved stature in many areas. Its College of Agriculture and several departments of the College of Arts and Sciences included faculty who were nationally and internationally recognized for their achievement.

Dr. Willard and his staff came to the University of Kentucky convinced that the best education for physicians and other health professionals required an academic orientation and a university setting. They brought a firm commitment to the concept of the Medical Center as an integral part of the University.

When they saw their dream for a Medical Center about to be realized, Dr. Brick Chambers, who had played such an important role in bringing it to fruition, along with some community physicians and some members of the Kentucky Medical Foundation wanted to locate the Medical Center on the Mount Vernon farm (later developed for housing) about a mile from the central campus. They envisioned relocating one or two of the existing community hospitals there, having office buildings for community physicians, all in addition to the facilities of the University's College of Medicine and Medical Center. Experiences elsewhere indicated that such a location would impose serious barriers to medical center - university integration. It has also been demonstrated that excessive reliance on hospitals that were not controlled by a medical college could compromise opportunities for flexibility and innovation in medical education. Dr. Willard was firm in his resolve that this was unacceptable and his position was upheld by the University Board of Trustees.

The site chosen for the Medical Center, a 39 acre segment of the College of Agriculture's 575 acre experimental farm, was contiguous with the central campus. Designation of this site meant that, in the future, the Medical Center would be within a short walk of the entire campus. Because this farm was gradually becoming surrounded by a growing city, plans were already afoot for replacing it with a farm in a more rural location.

Among the priorities of the planning staff was a need to become acquainted with as many of the University's administrators and faculty as quickly as possible. It was important to show respect for them and their concern for their University; to hear of their own aspirations and of their expectations for the Medical Center; to identify those who would be supporters and endeavor to assuage the fears of those who looked on the Medical Center with apprehension or mistrust; to identify some common goals; and to share some philosophy and aspirations. Some of this getting acquainted was carried out on a one by one basis. Fairly soon, however, members of the planning staff were invited to serve on various university committees. Although time consuming, this was an important and welcome symbol of "belonging" within the family and it afforded opportunities to meet more people and to develop a better appreciation of the rest of the University.

As in most Universities, academic governance at the University of Kentucky was vested in the faculty. At about the time of the establishment of the Medical Center, the faculty had become concerned with what they perceived as a duplication of certain types of course offerings by several departments or colleges. Statistics had been a major "offender." More than a dozen courses offered by different units were found to cover much of the same material. In an effort to eliminate waste and conserve resources, the faculty had adopted a policy called "departmental unity" designed to prevent the reoccurrence of such duplication. Under this policy no subject could be taught by more than one department in the University.

With the advent of a College of Medicine, there were a few subject areas for which the "departmental unity" policy became a issue. There was a department of bacteriology, chaired by a veterinarian, who was to insist for years that his department should be responsible for teaching microbiology to medical students. The incumbent chairman of the department of psychology wrote a letter to his Dean expressing the assumption that he and his colleagues should be responsible for recruiting the faculty who would teach psychiatry. Some faculty members who were advising pre-medical undergraduates assumed that they should be responsible for the admissions program of the College of Medicine. There was an existing department of anatomy and physiology, both basic science subjects for medical students, in the College of Arts and Sciences, and also a department of hygiene and public health and one of rehabilitation medicine. The future of all of these programs and their personnel posed questions that would need to be resolved. For the academic vice president of the

University, Dr. Leo Chamberlain, who had chaired the 1953 faculty committee that recommended a Medical Center, these and related issues of expansion and increasing complexity became very worrisome and perhaps even hastened his decision to retire.

Another area of stress and conflict, potential and real, was the business sector of the University directed by its Vice President, Dr. Frank D. Peterson. Dr. Peterson was openly uncomfortable with the arrangement that bypassed the University on architectural and construction contracts for the Medical Center and that permitted Dr. Willard to work directly with President Dickey and appropriate State officials in justifying and negotiating the Center's operating budget. In those areas pertaining to the Medical Center for which he retained responsibility, Dr. Peterson maintained strong control and there were many issues requiring conflict resolution.

THE SETTING - STATE GOVERNMENT

Former Governor A.B. "Happy" Chandler had long been interested in improving the level of health care for Kentuckians and had long supported the idea of creating a state supported medical school at the University of Kentucky. When he first began publicly preparing to run again for Governor in 1952 he identified the medical school as one of his anticipated campaign issues. It was a major issue in his successful bid for reelection in 1955. His recommendation for an initial appropriation of five million dollars was quickly approved by the General Assembly.

As Chairman of the Board of Trustees of the University of Kentucky during his term of office, Governor Chandler also played a key role in the selection and recruitment of Dr. Willard and in facilitating the removal of bureaucratic roadblocks that might well have impeded construction and activation. With few exceptions, such as the insistence that coal be used to fuel the Center's power plant, the Governor protected the Center from political interference. Some people feared that because the Center was so closely identified with Governor Chandler, it would not be supported by his successor. As will be noted later, Bert T. Combs, succeeded Chandler. Although he and Chandler had long been bitter political opponents, Combs gave the Medical Center his own full support and was primarily responsible for providing it with needed additional capital financing and with a very adequate initial operating budget. Governor Combs liked to say that Chandler had built the new Medical Center but that he had "paid for it."

A key figure in Frankfort during the Medical Center's development was the Director of the Department of Finance, Dr. James W. Martin. Dr. Martin had been borrowed for the job by Chandler from his position as Director of the Bureau of Business Research at the University of Kentucky. A man of absolute integrity and great wisdom, Jim Martin played a major role in facilitating the complex processes involved in design, construction and financing. He identified misjudgments, respected the need for quality, and was of immeasurable help in coordinating the various required approvals from the State and Federal governments. Dr. Martin assigned a member of his staff, Carl B. Delabar, to work essentially full time on the Medical Center planning. Later, Delabar was recruited by Dr. Willard and was to serve for nearly 30 years as the Medical Center's chief financial officer. Delabar and Martin were important advocates for the Medical Center when people examining the blueprints questioned the need for "luxuries" such as private offices for faculty, study cubicles and a lounge for medical students, a room for vending machines, doors on rest room booths, and the like.

Another source of support in Frankfort and statewide was Dr. Russell Teague, Director of the State Health Department. Because Dr. Teague was recognized and respected as one of the country's outstanding health officers, his support for the Medical Center carried considerable weight among public health professionals. His wise advice was also helpful in many ways.

LOUISVILLE'S INTERESTS

Major opposition to the Medical Center had been mounted by the Louisville *Courier-Journal* that was owned by the

Bingham family who were patrons of many good causes in Louisville including its University. In 1956, the Jefferson County Medical Society had overwhelmingly voted "disapproval" of a University of Kentucky Medical School. They were joined by many alumni of the Louisville Medical School who were practicing medicine throughout the State and by some members of Louisville's business and political contingent. On the "other side" were some forceful leaders like Dr. Samuel Overstreet, past President of the State Medical Society.

An editorial that appeared in the August 4, 1957 Lexington Sunday *Herald-Leader* exemplifies the issue. Responding to a *Courier-Journal* article by columnist Allan Trout that predicted a 29 million dollar shift from state surplus to deficit and blamed much of this on Governor Chandler's support of the Medical Center, the editorial accused Mr. Trout of "slanting his tax-scare article to meet the thinking of his Louisville bosses, who apparently cannot become reconciled to the establishment of a first-class medical school at UK."

The opposition of the Louisville establishment made the position of Dr. J. Murray Kinsman, Dean of the University of Louisville Medical School, particularly awkward yet courageous. While asserting that his school's survival depended on maintaining and increasing its level of state support, Dr. Kinsman stated that Louisville could not meet the State's need for more doctors and that he did not oppose the creation of a second medical school in Lexington. Before he agreed to accept the position in Kentucky, Dr. Willard went to Louisville to meet and consult with Dean Kinsman. The two Deans developed a mutual respect that served both schools well, particularly when they found themselves in competition for the best applicants to medical school, and when the media persisted in magnifying their rivalry.

THE SETTING - THE MEDICAL COMMUNITY

Once the decision to establish a medical school at the University of Kentucky was finalized, most of the overt opposition that had divided the medical community seemed to subside.

There continued to be some skeptics who questioned whether the State could muster the personnel and resources to make it a really good medical school and there were those who were apprehensive about competition from the school's projected clinical programs. However, by and large physicians and other health professionals "rallied 'round the cause." This was in part because, when he was being recruited and throughout the planning process, Dr. Willard established and maintained contact with medical leadership, not only in Fayette County but throughout the State. As part of the planning process, he and other members of his staff attended their meetings, provided an explanation of the planning objectives, responded to questions, and invited suggestions.

Credit is also due to the Kentucky Medical Foundation that lobbied both politically and with professional organizations on behalf of the College of Medicine and Medical Center. Although the Foundation did not achieve one of its goals - that of attracting significant amounts of private funding for the Center - it played a very effective role in stimulating professional and public interest and support. In addition, individual members of the Foundation continued to provide useful advice and encouragement and friendship during the hectic years of planning. As a tribute to their significant efforts that led to the establishment of the Medical Center and the creation of the Kentucky Medical Foundation, portraits of Drs. John Chambers, Coleman Johnston, Francis Massie and Edward Ray were hung in the foyer of the Medical Science Building. Also significant, though in a different and generally unrecognized way, was the supportive role of Dr. John P. Sprague. John Sprague was President of the Fayette County Medical Society in 1956 and was serving as surgeon for the University Health Service on a part-time basis. He and his wife Louise, quietly and unassumingly, befriended the planning staff families and helped them feel welcome in and adjust to their new community. John also became an informal confidant; a "sounding board" whose wise and thoughtful judgment was helpful on many occasions. Dr. Sprague eventually gave up his private practice and worked full-time with the University Health Service until his retirement.

THE SETTING - A PLACE TO WORK

As already noted, events moved very rapidly once the initial financing for and the formal establishment of the College of Medicine took place. Not only were Dr. Willard and his planning group members forced to fulfill prior commitments and uproot families on short notice, but they had to find a place to work and basic equipment to work with. Faced with a rapidly growing enrollment of students and little in the way of recent physical plant expansion, the University was literally "bursting at the seams" in the Fall of 1956. A small classroom in the Fine Arts Building was appropriated as an office for Dr. Willard and a secretary. The other four staff were initially installed in a recently excavated portion of the basement of the original King Library. Several assorted packing crates served as "desks" while the real things were being procured. The entrance was by means of an outdoor cellar stairway through a door that permitted people accidentally to be locked inside. This was a particularly stressful arrangement before a telephone was finally installed that permitted a call for help.

One advantage of the basement dungeon was that it provided strong motivation for staff members to escape by beginning to visit various parts of the State and to become acquainted on a first hand basis with the health personnel, resources and needs. Within a few months the staff was relocated in the Freeman House, a six room farm house that stood on the future site of the Medical Center just beyond the end of the current College of Dentistry wing. By this time the multifaceted planning process was well underway.

Chapter Four

THE PHILOSOPHY OF
MEDICAL EDUCATION

Even before arriving in Lexington, Dr. Willard and his planning staff had begun to formulate a position statement that could serve as a guide for the work ahead. This statement was further refined in response to the experience of the first few months in Kentucky. Then, in December of 1956 it was distributed as a formal statement of purpose. In some respect it is as relevant today as it was 40 years ago. It is certainly relevant to the history of the College of Medicine and is reproduced here in its entirety.

———————

A Philosophy of Medical Education
for the
University of Kentucky College of Medicine
Prepared by the U. of K. Medical Center Staff
December 15, 1956

Medicine is a study of human growth, development, and illness throughout the life span. It includes the biological, mental, emotional, social, and cultural factors that bear upon normal human development and its aberrations. It implies an integrative approach and denies the necessity for artificial separation between the traditional basic and clinical sciences or between undergraduate, professional and postgraduate education. Thus, medicine is as concerned with health and its preservation as with disease and its diagnosis and treatment.

The objective of the medical school program is to educate the "undifferentiated physican" - one grounded in the sciences of medicine and prepared, with further training, to engage in the practice of general medicine or any of its specialties. We do not believe the physician who has just finished medical school is prepared to practice medicine without further training in good internship and residency.

We believe that students should be imbued with the philosophy of family practice so that they consider patients as members of the family unit. The physician should serve as a family health advisor, treating those illnesses for which he is competent and coordinating the services of specialists when they are needed.

We believe further in the wisdom of collaborative work among physicians and that the isolated practitioner is handicapped in rendering quality services, in keeping abreast of new knowledge, and in being able to lead a reasonable life.

Medical Education in Ferment

There is a real ferment in medical education today. Medical educators are increasingly self critical of their programs and products, although the medical professional and medical educators usually have been pioneers in improving the quality of medical education. The present period of experimentation has been stimulated in part by the dramatic advances in medical science which make it increasingly difficult for the physician to know all that it would be desirable for him to know. It has been stimulated also by new knowledge of human behavior. This knowledge not only provides new material for the curriculum, but also offers the potentiality of improved teaching methods consonant with current knowledge of the psychology of learning. Experimentation has been occasioned also by changes in society and the methods by which medical care is offered. Medicine as an institution of society is finding its role changed with expanding opportunities to serve society and with greater expectations on the part of the public.

In planning a new program of medical education it is essential to be aware of this ferment, to know and evaluate the various experiments in process, to select that which seems good and relevant from the experimental programs while holding fast to tried and proven methods. It is also important to plan the facilities and program so that flexibility can be maintained. If this is done, the program can be adapted easily as additional improvements become possible.

The key elements in a program of medical education are: first, the student; second, the teacher; third, the patient. The laboratories, classrooms, the teaching hospital and clinic, the student dormitories are tools to facilitate the progress of education; they are not ends in themselves.

The Student

Increased emphasis should be placed upon selecting students who have qualities of character, personality and motivation for human service in the best tradition of the medical profession. Intellectual ability, essential as it is, cannot be considered sufficient in itself.

There are reasonably good methods for evaluating intellectual capacity, the best being the performance of the student in college, supplemented by certain psychological tests, such as the Medical College Admissions Test. The other important qualities are more difficult to measure but techniques are being developed by which motivation, interest patterns and personality can be determined more objectively and accurately than ever before.

Another important consideration, especially for Kentucky, is the selecting of students who are likely to remain in the State and serve the people in the small towns and rural areas.

These considerations call for an important investment in developing an admissions program which selects from among applicants on the basis of merit and willingness to serve the people of the State. Because there is much we do not know about selecting the best qualified applicants, the admissions program should include extensive research to evaluate its success and to improve the admissions activities of the future. Such a research program may yield results applicable to fields other than medicine.

The study of medicine is the preparation for a profession. The student should be considered as reasonably mature and adult; he should be treated as a responsible person able to exercise initiative and good judgment. With a minimum of supervision, students should govern themselves through a student organization. As members of a profession, the students should live under an honor system. Certain characteristics of an undergraduate school, such as enforced attendance at classes, should be conspicuous by their absence.

Not all students will be mature and self-sufficient. Many students will have problems and will need guidance and assistance.

The resources of the school should be developed to provide this help as needed. The University Health Service is especially important. Because it will serve future physicians and students with some sophistication in medicine, it must exemplify the best in medical practice. It should provide a learning experience as well as a medical service. Experience has demonstrated the need for adequate psychiatric service for students. There should be provided also adequate counseling service related to academic work and to various personal problems. Finally, there should be economic assistance for students in need, particularly loan and scholarship funds. All of these services are essential if society is to capitalize on its investment in the students selected for the study of medicine.

In our concern for the student, we must give particular attention to student life. We want physicians who are broadly educated, who take an interest in the affairs of the community and in cultural activities. We want responsible citizens, not narrow technicians, physicians who are personally well adjusted and therefore able to help others in need. As a generalization, we in medical education often say this and then we put students through a four-year program which makes it difficult, if not impossible, for them to develop these interests and qualifications. Cultural interests and social responsibility must be nurtured, but medical schools are often conducted in a way which makes this nurture impossible. Too often the student is confronted with a heavy curriculum and full schedule which permits no free time, no opportunity to engage in cultural pursuits or to participate in community affairs. We frequently place him under excessive anxiety by our examination program and grading system; we develop a competitive spirit rather than a cooperative spirit. In many schools, we do not provide adequate living facilities in which students can be reasonably comfortable and which permit good study habits and normal social or family life. For this reason dormitory and student centers are essential facilities.

The Teacher

The best teaching is by example, and therefore, it is incumbent upon the University to select teachers who have qualities of mind and character which students should emulate. The teacher must have a primary interest in students and teaching. Obviously, he must be competent in his subject, but also he should understand the psychology of learning and why people behave as they do. He should understand himself and how to use his talents most effectively.

Having selected teachers of promise, the University has an obligation to help these teachers improve themselves, their teaching methods, and their skills. The University must recognize good teaching in considering promotions. The salary and personnel policies should reward properly the work of its teachers and contribute to good morale. They should be designed to hold good faculty members.

This is not to minimize the importance of research. There is ample experience to indicate that the best teachers have an insatiable curiosity and maintain active research programs. The teaching load must be limited so that each faculty member has time for research. Moreover, the University should support financially a reasonable amount of research. Such support should include adequate laboratory space, equipment and supplies, and some technical and secretarial assistance. Although many faculty members can secure substantial research grants to underwrite the cost of their research, there is a level of continuing support which the University should supply.

Proper policies and practices in the selection, development and reward of its faculty will overcome the criticisms sometimes made of the full-time medical school teacher - that he is interested exclusively in his research, that he is disinterested in students, insensitive to their needs, and unable to teach effectively.

The Patient

The University Hospital and Out-Patient Clinic have their primary justification in advancing the program of education and research of the University. To teach students effectively the patients should exemplify the broad range of diseases. It is important also that students have experience with patients in differing economic and social levels. Accordingly, an admission policy for the University Hospital and Clinic which provides selectivity on the part of the University to advance the cause of teaching and research is important.

For the most part, however, the student and the teacher must learn to deal with patients as they come. The patient must be considered as an individual, with attention given to all of his problems. He must not be considered as a "case" or a collection of pathological processes. The operation of the institution and the educational program must be planned to demonstrate continuity of care and concern with the patient as a whole and as an individual having human dignity.

The Content of the Educational Program

A. The Traditional Medical Sciences

Because the physician must know a certain body of knowledge if he is to work efficiently, the content of the program is important. The program must give adequate emphasis to the traditional basic medical sciences, i.e., anatomy, physiology, biochemistry, pathology, microbiology, and pharmacology, as well as to the traditional clinical sciences, e.g., obstetrics and gynecology, pediatrics, psychiatry, medicine, and surgery. These remain today, as undoubtedly they always will, basic elements in the educational program. Important new knowledge is accumulating rapidly in all of these fields so that it becomes increasingly difficult to cover them adequately during the period of formal medical education.

B. The Behavioral Sciences and Administrative Medicine

There are, however, important new elements which need adequate representation in the curriculum. Prominent among these are the behavioral sciences which help the physician to understand the social and psychological determinants of behavior. These provide new insights and tools by which the physician can better understand the patient as a person. He can understand better the emotional overlay of organic illness, can differentiate the psychosomatic from the organic problems and deal with them. He can understand himself better and how to use his talents in dealing with the patient as an individual. He can appreciate better the social and cultural forces which may be causing or complicating the patient's illness and he can learn how to deal with such forces for the benefit of the patient.

Another new element is that of Administrative Medicine. Advances in the science of medicine, the demands and expectancies of the public for medical care, an expanding philosophy of social responsibility for the sick and disabled, and changes in society itself have resulted in new roles for the physician and new methods for providing medical care. More than ever before, medical care is being provided or financed through some form of social organization. The popular stereotype of the practicing physician as a solo practitioner, completely self-sufficient, is rarely true.

If the physician is to be successful and satisfied, if the medical profession is to meet the demands of society in providing personal health services, if health programs are to be effectively administered, then the young physicians must understand what is happening. They can acquire this best through a study of these developments presented in historical perspective, and through an adequate understanding of social organization for health services.

62

The concept of Comprehensive Medicine has emerged in recent years.

This term includes:
1. Preventive medicine
2. Diagnosis and treatment
3. Rehabilitation of the disabled

It also includes continuity of medical care over a period of time, in health as well as in sickness, and preferably with medical care provided for the patient or coordinated for him by the same physician. The practice of comprehensive medicine requires recognition of the interrelationships among physical, emotional, and psychological components of illness.

Too often medical care is episodic, fragmented among specialists and not coordinated. Prevention and rehabilitation are overlooked. These faults must be corrected, insofar as possible, in the institutions in which the students learn medicine. Formal teaching and example in the Medical Center must emphasize "comprehensive medicine."

The Educational Program

Although the faculty of the medical school must be responsible for establishing the curriculum and the teaching methods, there are certain policies which should be established in advance.

A. Medical Education Is a Life Long Process

The medical school program is not terminal education. It is followed by the internship and residency or by other forms of postgraduate and continuing education. Therefore, it is not necessary or wise to teach in medical school everything that a student might need to know. The program content must be selective, and the selection can vary among students to meet their individual needs.

B. Individual Instruction

The essence of individualized instruction which can meet the needs of students diverse in capacities and interests lies in small group teaching. Medicine has led the way in this kind of teaching, particularly in the clinical clerkship, but this approach has not been used as extensively in the basic medical sciences. Partly for ease and convenience, partly because of tradition and partly because of the nature of the work, the basic sciences have been taught primarily in large classes. In some programs, dividing the class into small discussion groups to supplement the lectures and laboratory work has been helpful in individualizing instruction. In other schools, project teaching using small groups is another example of individualizing instruction. Much more should be done in this direction.

It is well known that students learn and mature at different rates. Therefore, students should be allowed to progress at different rates through the medical curriculum. There is no reason why all students should take four academic years. Some will do much better in four and one-half or five years. A few may be able to do the work in less time than four years.

The curriculum should be organized to make some variation possible. The culture of the school should be developed so that variation is expected. The student who departs from the norm should not be penalized or stigmatized socially, intellectually, or financially (the latter by paying additional tuition).

C. Early Contact with Patients

Because the practice of medicine deals with living people and their problems, the student should be introduced to the study of people early in his professional education, preferably in the first year. He should understand the development of personality and behavior and the social and environmental forces to which people are subject, just as he must understand human biology. Formal teaching in this area can be re-enforced by appropriate "laboratory experience" in which the student has contact with patients. His role must be adequately defined as that of a student rather than a physican, and he must be given the necessary supervision and support. He must acquire a feeling of security and learn effective patterns of behavior from such an experience. His responsibility must be appropriate to his ability.

There is now evidence that the student's motivation can be enhanced and his effectiveness improved by such a program. We have tended to emphasize exclusively the traditional basic sciences during the first two years, shielding the student from an opportunity to understand and deal with people during this important period.

D. Free Time

The curriculum must be so organized and scheduled that students have some free time for independent work, electives and reading. Students need some "quiet time" in which to think and organize their knowledge. It is important also that students have an opportunity to live a reasonable life, indulging moderately their tastes in cultural activities and participating responsibly in their community. The academic year must not be scheduled so completely with classes and laboratories that this is impossible.

E. Laboratory Teaching

The objective of laboratory work is to enable the student to acquire essential technical skills, and to understand the scientific method. It should help him to understand better the concepts and principles developed in his course of work, and to determine his interest and aptitude for work in certain fields of medicine.

The required laboratory work should be that amount necessary to meet those objectives. It may not be necessary to do laboratory work in every subject field. That which is done should be organized largely around individual group projects, rather than around standardized "cook book" exercises. Much can be presented as demonstrations.

The reduction in scheduled laboratory hours is one way by which students can be granted more free time and the opportunity to do more independent work.

F. Concepts and Principles vs. Facts: the Scientific Method

The increasing mass of scientific knowledge poses difficult problems for the medical educator and student. The answer must lie in the teaching of concepts and principles. Obviously, the student must learn enough facts to deal with these concepts and principles effectively.

Rather than insist on memorizing an excessive number of facts, the student must be taught the use of tools by which he can supplement his knowledge of facts when necessary. The tools include reference books, journals, the library, the laboratory and consultants.

It is highly important for the student to learn the methods of science, how to formulate a hypothesis, how to test it with a controlled experiment, how to evaluate the results which he and others achieve from their experiments and from their clinical practice.

G. Audiovisual Aids

The development of audiovisual aids, particularly films and television, offers great promise for improving the effectiveness of teaching, and the program should be designed to take full advantage of these developments in educational method and technology.

II. Student Evaluation

The evaluation of students and their work will remain as an essential responsibility of the faculty. There are many ways in which this can be done and the techniques are being improved constantly. The purposes of evaluation and the characteristics to be evaluated must be clearly defined, and the most objective measures available should be used.

Examinations may be harmful, particularly if they are too frequent and carry too much weight in the evaluation of the student. They may place students under too much pressure, create harmful anxiety, result in competition among courses for student time, and interfere with opportunities the student may have for thinking, reading, and coordinating information.

Formal examinations should be minimal in number, perhaps limited to comprehensive examinations at the end of the year. They should require the integration of knowledge. This would not preclude occasional course examinations which the students could take voluntarily and which would not be recorded as part of the official evaluation of the student. These can help students gauge their progress and the faculty to evaluate their teaching. Such examinations must be used promptly as teaching exercises with the students.

The de-emphasis on examinations can be balanced by evaluating other activities, such as performance in the laboratory, in special projects, in working with patients, in analyzing their problems, and in writing their records.

I. Interdisciplinary Teaching and the Team Approach

As new knowledge has increased, the boundary lines between the different medical sciences have been crumbling. The pathologist is dependent upon the biochemist, and much of anatomical research now falls into the biochemical and physiological areas. The internist needs the services of the biophysicist, and all clinicians are increasingly concerned with the behavioral sciences. These in turn are turning to physiology and biochemistry increasingly. The traditional departmental boundaries afford a means for convenient administration of the medical school, but the teaching program should be largely interdisciplinary in character to help the student obtain a balanced view of the medical sciences and to integrate his knowledge. Similarly, many of the research activities of the faculty require an interdisciplinary approach. Accordingly, the program of the school must be structured to foster interdisciplinary teaching and research, and faculty must be selected who want to work with others, rather than in isolation.

Similarly, medical practice today requires the collaboration of many specialists in medicine and the assistance of many associated personnel, such as doctors, nurses, dentists, social workers, physiotherapists, vocational counsellors, and others. This calls for teamwork in patient care, but unfortunately the physician is too seldom able to work as a member of a team. He is made the captain of the team, and yet he exemplifies too seldom the characteristics that make for a good team leader. The program of medical education must be so designed that effective teamwork is the accepted way of work. The student should see by example what teamwork means. The program must provide him also with an opportunity to understand the functions of the other members of the team, the educational programs for training such personnel, the kinds of people who enter these occupations, and their need for understanding and recognition.

The Medical School and the University

Since the Flexner Report early in this century, medical education has been accepted as a university function. The university has much to offer the medical school, and in return, the medical school has much to offer the university. We believe that this must be exemplified at the University of Kentucky to justify university sponsorship of medical education.

As previously pointed out, medical science has broadened its horizons to recognize the relevance of the behavioral sciences. Many of these are not discrete subjects for the medical curriculum, but they are pertinent to the teaching and research program. They are especially relevant to a broad and liberal education, deemed essential for a modern physician.

The medical school cannot and should not hope to develop all of these fields itself. As a member of the university family, however, it can call upon these resources elsewhere in the university.

In a similar way, the resources of the medical school should be available to enrich and broaden the subject area content of related fields within the university, such as chemistry and biology and the behavioral sciences.

If education is to be viewed as a continuum for the student, it is highly important for the teachers of the undergraduate student and those of the professional school to give common thought to the development of an integrated educational experience. Certainly, this can be accomplished best within the framework of a university.

The concept of a health team is assuming increasing importance. It is important for the doctor to understand the philosophy and educational program of the nurse, laboratory technician, physiotherapist, clinical psychologist, and other health workers, to know what to expect of these colleagues and how to work with them effectively. These are programs offered frequently by the university, and a good opportunity is afforded to develop educational programs and relationships cooperatively and to facilitate teamwork. Frequently it is too late if this is left entirely for the professional school.

If the professional student is to be encouraged to develop his cultural interests even while in medical school, what better place is there than the university campus? Also, he has access to recreational facilities of the university and other resources with which to enrich his life. Too frequently these are not utilized effectively, but this is a criticism of either the individual or the program and not the opportunity.

The medical school and its faculty have the responsibility of citizenship within the university community. They must participate in educational and university planning. If asked, they should give guidance in fields of their competence, such as the provision of health and other clinical service, but this does not mean necessarily that they have the responsibility for providing these services personally.

The Medical School and the Community

The medical school is an institution of society created to satisfy certain social needs. As an educational institution its functions are defined primarily as teaching and research. It prepares people to provide medical services and seeks new knowledge to prevent, cure and alleviate disease. These are enduring responsibilities. However, as the health problems of society change, the character of the educational and research programs must change to meet them.

The medical school must know what the health problems of society are and the factors - biological, sociological, cultural and economic - which cause or contribute to them. These will differ to some extent from one area to another. Because change is constant, study of these problems and factors must be constant.

If health needs are to be met, the necessary services must

reach people. In our complex society, health services are being given increasingly through some form of social organization. There are many examples which historically are relatively recent, such as the modern hospital, health and welfare departments, industrial medical services, and pre-payment insurance plans. As our concepts of social responsibility are broadening, the character of programs provided by social institutions is greatly influenced.

Some physicians do not understand in historical perspective what is happening in the social organization for medical services. Some are unfamiliar with available resources and do not know how to use them for the benefit of their patients, nor do they know how to work effectively with those responsible for the administration of health programs.

Much improvement is needed in the administration of medical services. Despite this need, there is a serious shortage of physicians and other personnel trained to administer health programs. In fact, the environment in some educational institutions tends to depreciate the administrator and discourage physicians and other able people from considering this kind of work as a worthy career.

The role of a medical school appears clear from these considerations. To know the health problems of the area, some members of the faculty must study them. They must study also the administration of health services and delineate the problems which obstruct the provision of necessary and desired services. To accomplish this, the community must be utilized as a laboratory in which the medical school studies certain problems, just as the hospital ward or physiology laboratory must be utilized for the study of other problems.

Since the best teaching is by example, it is important for the student to observe and participate in the study of community health problems and to assist in the provision of community health services. This can be done satisfactorily only if the community has well developed programs of comprehensive scope. Thus, it becomes important for the medical school to help the community develop such services in the programs to which it has access, just as it is important for the medical school to develop an

71

efficient and broad range of services in the teaching hospital.

In this the medical school becomes a resource to help the community define its problems and devise ways of meeting them, and the community becomes a resource to help the medical school train people for administrative and policy making positions in health agencies.

Chapter Five

BECOMING

September 1956 thru August 1960

Convinced that the development
of the Medical Center must be guided by a set of clearly stated
objectives, Dr. Willard made the delineation of a philosophy of
medical education the first priority for his planning group. This
statement became a guiding basis for a wide variety of decisions
involving building design, curriculum, and patient care. It served
as a basis for explaining the Medical Center and its goals and
objectives to state officials in Frankfort, administrators and faculty of the University, members of the health professions and citizens groups throughout the Commonwealth. It also proved of
great value in the process of recruiting the initial cadre of department chairs and other key faculty members. This chapter will
review the process of moving from a set of objectives to the
College's becoming a reality with the admission of its first students
in the fall of 1960.

Upon arrival in Lexington in the fall of 1956, members of
the planning staff were faced with a long list of priorities each of
which seemed critical. Because there were clearly "not enough

hours in a day," we worked nights as well. Inspired by Dr. Willard's own example and stimulated by the opportunities and the challenges, we all drove ourselves without mercy. A typical day might start with a staff meeting at 6 a.m. and not end until late in the evening. We also were traveling a great deal visiting other university medical centers and, within Kentucky, trying to learn as much as possible about the needs and expectations of Kentucky's people. With grant applications or other deadlines upon us, I remember several occasions when I took time out at around 8 in the evening to drive home for an hour or so, kiss Ruth and our children and then go back to work for the rest of the night.

Bill Willard's own schedule put him in an awkward dilemma with respect to his membership in the Rotary Club that he had transferred from New Haven to Syracuse and on to Lexington. Rotary members were expected to attend a weekly meeting either at their own chapter or wherever they might be. Rotary chapters were rated on the basis of their members' attendance record. Bill found that the demands of his job were such that he simply could not meet this expectation and, rather than have the Lexington chapter lose credits on his account, he resigned. For this he was never quite forgiven by many of his fellow Rotarians, some of whom were community leaders. They considered his resignation an affront. As one member expressed his indignation to me: "No one should ever resign from the Rotary." It was a no win situation for Dr. Willard for either way he went he stood to lose the support of those who took their Rotary membership and its obligations very seriously.

Although Dr. Willard felt that it was important for all staff members to have a general familiarity with the whole process, quite quickly they assumed a division of labor. Howard Bost had the major responsibility with respect to financing the construction and equipping of the Center. To this end he worked closely with both the Department of Finance in Frankfort and granting agencies in Washington. He and Alan Ross did several studies on individual's and families' access to and financing of health care including a study on how the faculty and staff of the University of Kentucky were meeting their own health care needs. They also worked closely with Russell White and the Kentucky Medical Foundation in connection with their efforts to provide a positive image and solicit significant private financial support for the Center. As the hospital was being designed, their studies of experiences elsewhere led to the pioneering of the concept of progressive patient care. Howard Bost also designed the physician's practice plan that will be discussed later. Bost's expertise in health care economics was quickly recognized and respected. He and Dr. Willard soon found themselves asked to consult with numerous governmental departments and agencies throughout the State that were concerned with health issues.

Alan Ross brought a broad scholarly background, rigorous statistical training and an analytical mind to the planning process. He had an uncanny ability to ask the right questions, did not hesitate to tell us that "the king isn't wearing any clothes," and was a valuable problem solver in many areas.

Dick Noback focused on the physical features of buildings that would facilitate the achievement of philosophical goals. He studied the design of numerous other medical schools and hospitals and then worked closely with the architects on many details of design especially for laboratories in the basic science building and for patient care areas of the hospital. Prior to the recruitment of a Dean and staff to plan the College of Dentistry, Noback became the chief "specialist" in dental education. When, within a few months, responsibility for the University's Student Health Service was transferred to the Medical Center staff, Noback was given major responsibility for this and eventually served as its Director. During the transition toward activation of the clinical programs he also served briefly as Coordinator of Clinical Affairs.

Robert Straus became the staff specialist on curriculum for the College of Medicine and on developing a program for medical student selection and admissions. The curriculum and admissions jobs involved travel to explore the experiences at about twenty other medical schools, while the admissions role involved getting to know premedical advisors in colleges throughout Kentucky. Because I was given a faculty appointment in the College of Arts and Sciences' Department of Sociology as well as in the College of

Medicine, I also became the medical planning staff's most frequent representative on various University-wide committees. These roles afforded an opportunity to try to convince some of the more pessimistic faculty and administrators that the Medical Center would not doom the rest of the University to perpetual mediocrity and to encourage the continuing friendship and confidence of those who had supported the Medical Center all along.

Bill Willard was involved in all of these activities and with maintaining contact and negotiating with top level administration in both the University and the State Government. He also was participating in considerations of medical education at the national level. This gave him a perspective that would be helpful in assuring that the College of Medicine would qualify for accreditation when the time came. He and Noback played the major initial role in presenting the goals and objectives of the Center to the physicians of the State paving the way for an eventual pattern of cooperation, affiliation and referrals.

Among the most glaring deficiencies of existing university medical centers in the mid-1950s were a lack of space and facilities for medical education in "teaching" hospitals and a geographic separation of the hospitals from the rest of their medical schools. Therefore, one of the early decisions at Kentucky was to integrate the hospital with the rest of the medical center and to design the hospital with ample provisions for education. This meant that planning for the hospital had to be coordinated with that for the entire medical center, even though the construction and activation of the hospital would follow that of the medical science building by about two years. With this goal in mind, the first addition to the planning staff was Richard D. Wittrup who, in December 1956, was recruited from the University of Chicago Clinics with the expectation that he would become the future hospital's chief administrator.

Another high priority was to have a Medical Library developed and functioning as early as possible, not only as a resource for future students but as an essential factor in the recruitment of faculty. Obviously, the development of a library's collections would take many years. The next key appointment was the

Medical Librarian, Alfred N. Brandon, who came to Kentucky from the College of Medical Evangelists in Loma Linda, California. It would be hard to conceive of a more fortunate choice. Al Brandon not only knew what was required to develop a fine medical library, he knew how to go about it and he obviously had friends in high places within the world of medical librarians. He arrived in Lexington in a station wagon loaded with what became known as his "dowry"; hundreds of volumes that he had collected from other medical libraries on his trip across the country.

DECISIONS ABOUT DESIGN

One of the most pressing priorities was to make sure that the plans developed by the consulting architects would be consistent with the College's and the Medical Center's philosophy and goals. Because of the time required for design, approvals, applications for federal funding, bidding, selecting a contractor, constructing, equipping and activating the physical facilities, architectural planning had to assume a top priority. Initially, this meant planning the basic science facility where the first two years of curriculum would be taught and where administration and faculty offices and research laboratories would be located. Immediately thereafter, it would mean designing the hospital and also the facilities for a dental college.

The consulting architects, Ellerby and Company, proved to be a fortunate choice for several reasons. They were specialists in the design of medical facilities. They were in the process of completing work on a new College of Medicine and Medical Center for the University of Florida. There, they had worked with the Dean, Dr. George Harrell, a medical statesman and educator who shared many of Bill Willard's convictions. The Ellerby company was an architectural firm that gave close attention to function and believed that form should be adapted to the purposes of a project. This was in sharp contrast to the experience of a leading west coast University in the late 1950s. There, one of the nation's most prestigious architects had designed a medical center giving priority to form and fitting functions in as best he could. The result was a functional nightmare, major parts of which were so unusable for their intended purpose that they soon had to be replaced.

The Ellerby people also became intellectually involved in the philosophical objectives for the Center. They assigned one of their colleagues, Donald Nelson, to work virtually full time on the Kentucky project. Nelson moved his family to Lexington and worked side by side with the planning group. He often went along on visits to other medical schools to examine particular features of design and to hear answers to the standard question "what would you do differently if you had the chance?"

Numerous architectural decisions reflected the statement of philosophy. In order to facilitate close cooperation between programs and as much integration as possible, all units of the Medical Center were designed to be corridor connected and under a single roof. Other decisions flowing from philosophy included providing well furnished study and lounge space for students, showers in a rest room, and a convenient snack bar; providing rooms for small group teaching as well as lectures; installing one-way glass in several areas to facilitate the teaching of communication skills and to demonstrate respect for patient privacy (this was before it was feasible to use TV for these purposes); designing for students their own multipurpose laboratories to which faculty members from several departments would come to teach their particular topics (rather than have students go to the faculty); providing seminar space in each laboratory area; and providing facilities for programs in the behavioral sciences and community medicine, subjects that prior to that time had not traditionally been included in medical education.

The basic science building initially contained facilities for the College of Nursing. This location was intended to facilitate the integration of some aspects of basic science and clinical learning for nursing and medical students. However, with the arrival of a nursing college dean and faculty, the concept was rejected by them before it could ever be tried on the grounds that their students should have as much of their education as possible within the general university. The nursing faculty also rejected any role for physicians in the education of nursing students along with the concept of joint learning experiences for nursing and medical students. (After two or three years, the College of Nursing did turn to the College of Medicine's basic science Departments of Anatomy, Physiology and Behavioral Science to develop courses specifically for their students.) The initial location of space for nursing education had practical value in that it made portions of the medical science building eligible for federal grant support under the Hill-Burton Act.

In the design of facilities for the College of Medicine and the Medical Center some decisions to deviate from the traditional were based on the experiences of programs where innovations had already been tried. Some reflected the prevailing thinking of respected medical statesmen regarding what medical education in the last half of the 20th century should be. Most often they represented the opportunity afforded at the University of Kentucky to begin with basic objectives and develop programs and facilities which would be forward thinking, flexible, and a credit to the University and the Commonwealth while, at the same time, responding to the particular needs that the Medical Center was created to meet.

RELATING TO THE UNIVERSITY

While architectural decisions demanded a high priority, the pressure to cover numerous other fronts at the same time did not diminish. Obvious among these was the need to develop a spirit of trust and constructive collaboration with the parent University. Of special significance here was the mutual respect for each other that Dr. Willard and President Dickey shared. This overrode many obstacles. The Board of Trustees also responded well to Dr. Willard's presentations of purpose and President Dickey made sure that the Board had an opportunity to hear from Willard directly whenever this seemed important and relevant.

In July 1957, President Dickey arranged a convocation so that the entire University faculty and staff could hear a "progress report" on the Medical Center's planning and development. A major point emphasized at this meeting was the anticipation "that the Medical Center can achieve a degree of collaboration and integration within the framework of the University that will be more significant than that found in most Universities having medical schools." It was also stressed that the Medical Center staff hoped to "add strength and derive strength from the University at large."

Within the University at large two major issues of contention were apparent. One that has already been mentioned was a fear that the Medical Center would absorb all of the new resources for the University, leaving everyone else to struggle along in institutional poverty. The history of the State's modest financial support for the University up to that time supported such fears. The opposite view, fortunately held by many of the faculty's most distinguished members, was that the Medical Center would provide by example a wedge for raising the support for the rest of the University to an appropriate level. While it was possible to assure some of the fearful that the Medical Center staff were working for the best interests of the whole University, some of the apprehension and resentment was tenacious. (Some remained even after the financial support for and the stature of the University reached new heights in the mid-1960s.)

A second major issue in intra-University relationships was that of control; administrative, financial and academic. Because medical education represented an entirely new venture for the University, there were many areas of ambiguity. For example, whereas President Frank Dickey fully supported Dr. Willard and the planning group in their negotiations with the appropriate offices of State government regarding capital construction and later approved their operating budget proposals, to some others in the University this loss of control was threatening. As a result, after funds were allocated to the University for the Medical Center, there were frequent internal delays, requests for rejustification, and efforts to place limitations on their use. As time went by, this pattern of "antagonistic cooperation" was experienced particularly with respect to the selection and purchasing of certain types of technical equipment, the classification of personnel, and issues of control of hospital management and operation. It also was reflected in a redesignation of the Medical Center's site boundaries with the result that the Center is now split by Rose Street, a major traffic artery.

With respect to academic matters, there were a few faculty members who believed that the policy called "departmental unity," gave them the prerogative to assume academic responsibilities within the College of Medicine. Because of their very traditional and conservative concept of medical education this posed a potential problem. While relatively few in number, these individuals tended to be astute academic politicians and found some support in those who either feared the impact of the Medical Center on the University, or merely had a tendency to distrust "outsiders."

On the positive side, except when specific issues were raised, a majority of the University's faculty members and administrators respected and supported the Medical Center's development. Many expressed their anticipation of the time when they could themselves look to the Center for their own medical care. When, in 1957, the Medical Center assumed responsibility for the University's Student Health Service, it was possible, despite the Service's antiquated facilities, to demonstrate some improvements in quality of care, while retaining the support of Health Center personnel. Within a few months after arriving in Lexington, all members of the planning staff had been invited to participate in University and community activities by providing talks or lectures, serving on committees or boards, or being consulted about matters in which they were perceived to have some expertise.

My own experience is illustrative. In addition to offering me a joint appointment, several of the sociology faculty invited me to provide guest lectures for their classes and the Department suggested that I teach my own course whenever I felt I could. In 1957, I started a graduate course called Society and Health that is still being offered today. Among the several campus-wide committees on which I served was one that was asked by Blanton Collier, the football coach, to consider the impact of cloistering athletes in their own dormitory. Collier's players had their own

"Wildcat Lodge" but he was concerned that the isolation of his team from other students could have a negative impact on their education and overall college experience. Collier was forty years ahead of his time on this issue. It would not be until 1995 that the NCAA would finally forbid this practice.

There were also invitations to join the boards of health-related voluntary community agencies. I raised some eyebrows by indicating an interest in Planned Parenthood (an agency that I had served with in Syracuse) because in 1956 membership on the Lexington Planned Parenthood Board was restricted to women. I did join and eventually chaired the Board of the Family Counseling Service. Because my published research on drinking behavior and alcohol problems had received some national attention that followed us to Lexington, I received several requests from within the University, the Lexington community and across the State to be a speaker, serve on a committee or provide advice about alcohol related issues. There were also fairly frequent middle-of-the-night help seeking phone calls from alcoholics or their desperate family members.

In terms of its sheer magnitude and cost, the Medical Center was a far bigger undertaking than anything previously experienced by the University of Kentucky. In order to meet the needs of students and patients and serve the people of Kentucky well, and in order to be an asset in the recruitment of a well qualified faculty, the facility would have to be adequate in size, furnished with the most up-to-date equipment, and aesthetically pleasing. At the same time it was important to remember that Kentucky was a relatively poor state and that a significant portion of its people were living in conditions of poverty. Even Lexington, although it was a relatively affluent community, had pockets of extreme poverty, most of which were invisible to persons who traveled the main streets of town. These conditions demanded that every dollar the State was investing in the Medical Center be carefully spent.

The University of Kentucky was suffering its own form of poverty reflected in low salaries and Spartan conditions for teaching and working. Several departments were housed in surplus

World War II Army barracks that had been obtained in the mid-1940s as a "temporary" measure to meet the crunch of post-war enrollment. One of these structures, built with dried-out, partially finished lumber, was so dilapidated that it had become known as "splinter hall." Several faculty members with offices in "splinter hall" had resorted to carrying their research data home at night for fear that it would be destroyed by fire. There were other departments housed in equally fire prone buildings or former residences where working areas were crowded into hallways, kitchens and even closets. Although "splinter hall" survived to "meet the wreckers ball," a similar structure and one of the converted houses on the campus were subsequently destroyed by fires. Given these conditions, there was understandable sensitivity about the intention to provide in the Medical Center private offices with telephones, not only for faculty members but for some support staff as well. Facilities for students to study on the main campus were also very limited. Yet, plans for the Medical Center would include individual study cubicles for students along with other amenities.

Given this setting, it was critical that in planning the Medical Center, every effort be made to design facilities that would assure quality, provide for basic needs and be aesthetically pleasing while avoiding waste and excess. It was also necessary to achieve this within the limits of available resources at a time when neither the extent of potential resources or the costs of construction and equipment could be precisely determined. (This was one of the challenges that Dr. Willard described when he was asked why in the world he needed an economist and a statistician on his planning staff.)

IMPACT ON THE COMMUNITY

There were mixed feelings within the Lexington community about the coming of the Medical Center. On the one hand there were a sense of pride, an expectation that the Center would contribute to the community's stature, an anticipation that more local youth could become doctors and that the availability of quality medical care would be increased, and recognition that the Center would contribute significantly to the community's economy. On the other hand, there were concerns that the community was becoming too big or at least was growing too fast, that the people added to the community by the Center would create pressure for housing, schools and already burdened public services, and that too many outsiders would threaten the community's comfortable lifestyle. Within the health professions there was also ambivalence. Many welcomed the intellectual stimulation and professional support that the Center could bring and looked forward to participation in medical education both as teachers and continuing learners. At the same time there was apprehension among both practitioners and hospitals over the impact of new competition for patients.

Within the larger community, concerns were magnified by the fact that, coincidental with planning for the Medical Center, the International Business Machine Corporation was preparing to move its electric typewriter manufacturing unit from New York State to Lexington where it was expecting eventually to employ 6,000 people. When members of the medical center planning group sought housing in Lexington they found that the market was "tight." Few choices were available and they were competing with prospective IBM employees who had the advantage of well organized company assistance in finding and purchasing their homes.

It soon became apparent that it would be in the Medical Center's best interest to project its own impact on the community and to make such projections well known with the hope that the community would be able to plan its housing, schools, roads, fire houses and other resources accordingly. Such preparedness would be a crucial factor when the time came to recruit faculty and staff in large numbers and attract them to move to Lexington. To this end, one of Alan Ross's early assignments was to estimate the eventual impact of the Medical Center on the population and economy of Lexington. He had first to project the number of people who would be enrolled in or employed by the Medical Center by the mid-1960s and beyond. He then had to consider the impact of these new people and their families on the number of additional people and their families who would be employed to service their cars, deliver their mail, sell them groceries and in every other way meet their service and retail needs. Technically, this kind of projection can be extended to infinity. However, Alan was able to offer a reasoned estimate that the Medical Center, when fully developed, would add about 25,000 adults and children to the greater Lexington population and a substantial increment to the Lexington economy.

If the memoranda that included Ross' projections still exist, I have not been able to find copies in the archives. The figure of 25,000 people stands out in my memory. This is undoubtedly a significant underestimate because at the time, the Colleges of Allied Health and Pharmacy and the several large research centers such as those for Cancer and Aging were not included while the eventual dimensions of grant supported research and the outpatient clinic programs were not even dreamed of. In 1985, the University's Center for Business and Economic Research, under a contract with the Medical Center, conducted a study of the Medical Center's social and economic impacts on the State. The findings, both in scope of factors considered and magnitude of impact, go far beyond Ross's original projections. (See: Carol M. Straus et al, *The University of Kentucky Medical Center: Social and Economic Impacts*, Lexington: Center for Business and Economic Research, 1986 and Carol M. Straus, "Human Capital and the University of Kentucky Medical Center", in *Kentucky Economy: Review and Perspective*, Vol. 10, No. 1, Spring 1986, pp.10-14.)

In generating community support for the Medical Center and also in moderating community concerns, Dr. Willard was a remarkable ambassador. He took the initiative in seeking out community leaders both to inform them of his goals and to solicit expression of their concerns. Whenever possible, he responded to requests to meet with or talk to local groups. In all of these contacts, his clear and forthright discussion of goals and expectations for the Medical Center and its impact on the University, the Lexington community and the State, combined with his respect and concern for the concerns of others, inspired confidence and tended to allay fears.

Another ambassador, unpaid but not unappreciated, was Bill's wife. Adalyn Willard became a tireless worker for good causes within the community earning the several awards and recognitions that she received including one as "Lexington's Outstanding Woman." Adalyn managed to devote many hours a week to her civic activities while at the same time maintaining a large household for their three daughters and two elderly family members and giving frequent dinner parties and other forms of hospitality in support of Bill's professional work.

As one indication of Bill Willard's effectiveness as an ambassador, the Louisville *Courier-Journal*, that had vigorously opposed establishing a state supported medical school, revised its position. In May 1959, the paper published a series of feature articles by science editor Robert P. Clark that provided a very positive picture of the school's basic objectives and its plans for meeting them. This apparently met with the publisher's approval, for Clark was soon promoted to be Editor of the afternoon Louisville *Times*.

The generation of community support was by no means limited to Lexington, Louisville or Frankfort. Dr. Willard and members of his staff covered the State addressing county medical societies and other community groups, visiting hospitals and conferring with officials. This activity had a dual purpose. It provided opportunities to learn about varied health needs and potential sources of future collaboration. It also enabled the staff to share their goals and aspirations with the general public and with health professionals.

Of many trips that were made to various parts of Kentucky in order to meet people and learn about existing health resources and health needs, I remember particularly a visit to the Frontier Nursing Service in Leslie County that Howard Bost, Ed Pellegrino and I made in the winter of 1959. Established in 1925 by Mary Breckenridge to provide obstetrical and other medical care for the isolated people living in the mountains of Eastern Kentucky, the FNS had become famous for its nurses on horseback who maintained a number of clinics in very remote areas as satellites of a small hospital in Hyden. When the FNS was first established the nearest paved road was 60 miles away. In 1959, the drive from Lexington to Leslie County took about five hours and the FNS clinics were still located by creekbeds or mountain pathways. We were directed to a small garage standing on stilts over a ravine at the side of a rural road. There we were met by Mrs. Breckenridge's assistant Helen Browne, our car was left in the garage, and we were transported by jeep into and along a running stream to the FNS headquarters at Wendover. Wendover was an imposing log house where Mrs. Breckenridge and her key assistants lived and from which the FNS was administered. We were treated to a delicious dinner and a lengthy discourse on the history and current status of the FNS. Mary Breckenridge was well aware that the FNS would have to adapt to rapid and drastic changes. They had already substituted jeeps for horses on many of their routes and they saw the coming impact of paved roads. Already, with a few roads, the area was beginning to develop consolidated schools and some farmers were finding that they could share a "consolidated" bull. The FNS was looking toward the consolidation of their remote outposts and the opportunity to bring a more comprehensive form of health care to the people they served. Our discussion of "modernization" was interrupted by a messenger who reported that a water crisis was developing at the FNS hospital in Hyden. Mrs. Breckenridge's decisive response was "Send for Walter." Walter was the local water diviner. That night, with the outside temperature well below zero, we each slept in a luxurious feather bed further warmed by a fireplace that was fed throughout the night. The next morning, in addition to touring the hospital, we gathered outside on the hillside as Walter with his divining rod successfully demonstrated his skill.

CONCERN FOR THE MEDICALLY INDIGENT

Shortly after arriving in Kentucky, members of the planning staff were drawn into the consideration of a number of statewide health related activities that were quite distinct from but relevant to the creation of a university medical center. They were thus able to provide stimulation and leadership with respect to several issues of health care economics and delivery. For example, several of the studies that had identified the need for a medical school at the University of Kentucky had referred to the lack of provisions in the State for the medically indigent and suggested that this problem needed study and remedy. Accordingly, in late 1956 Governor Chandler appointed a Commission on the Study of Medical Care for the Indigent. The Commission was chaired by Dr. Russell E. Teague, Kentucky's outstanding Commissioner of Health. Dr. Willard was one of its 12 members and Howard Bost, as a member of its research staff, was responsible for writing its report.

There were a number of interests in the State at that time who looked upon the proposed University Hospital as a way to meet two needs at the same time; provide education for future doctors and "take care of" the problems of the medically indigent. Experiences elsewhere demonstrated that such a charity hospital could not provide the broad range of experiences needed for medical education and could serve only a fraction of the State's far-flung medically indigent population and meet only a portion of their varied health needs. The Commission quickly dismissed this simplistic approach and developed instead a series of recommendations that were to have far-reaching significance.

The Commission found that at that time, 1957, at least one out of every eight Kentuckians or 400,000 individuals were unable to pay for necessary medical care. They either had to depend on services provided free by physicians, hospitals or others or they had to go without medical care. The costs of "free" services were being met by higher fees charged to the sick who could pay for their own care. At the same time, many of those in need went without needed care because through pride or ignorance they failed to seek free services. Finding the prevailing practices both inequitable and inadequate, the Commission recommended a program that would provide state support to enable existing institutions and health care providers in all communities throughout the state to offer health care to the indigent. This plan had the effect of spreading the costs of medical care for the indigent among all taxpayers, increasing the availability of services to all persons in need, and enabling existing resources to expand and improve their services. It also helped to address the shortage of health care resources in rural areas. The Commission's recommendations were substantially implemented during the administration of Governor Bert Combs and they were to provide a model for other states and subsequent federal legislation. (See "A Long-Range Plan for Medical Care for Indigent Persons in Kentucky," A Report of the Governor's Commission on the Study of Medical Care for the Indigent, Frankfort, Ky., Oct. 25, 1957.)

SOME ORGANIZATIONAL ISSUES

Ever since the transformation of medical education that followed the Flexner Report of 1910, medical schools in the United States and Canada had been organized into basic science departments that were primarily responsible for the first two years of the curriculum and clinical departments that covered the last two years and provided training for interns and residents. The traditional basic science departments were anatomy, physiology, microbiology, biochemistry, pharmacology and pathology (also a clinical subject). These followed what had been fairly discrete discipline identities in the early decades of the 20th century. They also reflected a bias that only biological knowledge was basic to medicine, a bias that was associated with the dramatic discoveries in the biological sciences during the latter part of the 19th century that revolutionized medical theory and enormously enhanced the ability of physicians to cure disease.

The organization of clinical faculties followed a very old tradition of separating doctors into physicians (medicine) and surgeons (surgery). More recently, departments were developed for specialties dealing with children (pediatrics), the reproductive functions of women (obstetrics and gynecology), diseases of the mind (psychiatry), the nervous system (neurology), the provision of safe anesthesia (anesthesiology) and diagnostic techniques (pathology and radiology). As these various specialties became more focused, the overall health care of patients and concern about the interrelatedness of various aspects of their health became less focused.

By the 1950s discomfort with the traditional organization of medical school education was being expressed in occasional reports and articles and was reflected in a few experiments in medical education, most notably that of Western Reserve University where the curriculum had been organized around organ systems rather than departments. In its initial thinking, the planning staff at Kentucky favored abandoning a departmental structure for the College of Medicine's faculty, substituting instead a division for basic sciences and a clinical division. It was reasoned that the traditional basic science disciplinary boundaries were anachronistic both in terms of the current state of knowledge and the organization of research questions and projects. It was observed in other medical schools that, despite their discipline labels, there were no longer "pure" basic science departments; that, for example, it was common to find departments of anatomy that included physiologists, departments of physiology that included biochemists and departments of biochemistry that might include a pharmacologist, a physiologist and a microbiologist. Nor were there any longer many courses being taught or research projects being conducted or proposed that relied rigidly on only one of the traditional disciplines.

For a clinical faculty, the planning staff reasoned that a traditional departmental organization and orientation tended to encourage the fragmentation of patient care and a patient's problems. In a medical school that was committed to comprehensive medicine and to the education of primary physicians who would be expert in diagnosing the problems of their patients, providing care within their competence, making appropriate referrals to specialists and coordinating the total care of their patients, the fragmentation of learning according to the traditional specialty departments could be counterproductive.

Serious consideration of a non-departmental structure for the College of Medicine's faculty was carried into early discussions with respected medical educators at other schools and with persons who were recommended as potential key faculty at Kentucky.

While the concept was received with interest on a philosophical basis, it was overwhelmingly rejected for pragmatic reasons. We were told, and reluctantly became convinced, that there were simply not enough potential faculty members who would be willing to risk coming to a new medical school at the University of Kentucky into a structure that denied them the security of a departmental affiliation. Departments represented powerful political entities within universities and were important symbols of identity and acceptance within the professions.

Instead of deviating from a departmental structure, the planning group hoped that the interdigitation of the basic science disciplines could be accommodated in the organization of the curriculum and the educational goals for primary physicians could be built into the organization of patient care in the hospital and clinics. The development of the initial curriculum and patient care plans for the College will be discussed later. In addition, the medical science building was designed with the offices and research laboratories of basic science and clinical departments so located that faculty members would cross paths with those from other departments many times a day in hallways, stairwells, elevators and even rest rooms. It was hoped that the physical proximity of their working areas would facilitate communication and collaboration among faculty from different disciplines and departments.

As time went on, I became more convinced that the power vested in discipline oriented University departments was a major impediment to change in University curricula and a detriment to the advancement of knowledge. A paper on this topic, published by *Science* in 1973, elicited more than 50 letters to the editor or to me and more than 200 requests for reprints. Most respondents either strongly agreed or strongly disagreed with my thesis. One school dedicated an all day faculty retreat to the topic. The issue continues to be timely and the paper was reprinted by another journal in 1994. R. Straus "Departments and Disciplines: Stasis and Change," *Science*, Vol. 182, pp 895-898, 30 Nov. 1973; reprinted in *Annals of Behavioral Science and Medical Education*, Vol 1, pp 14-18, Spring 1994.

PLANNING FOR A FULL TIME FACULTY

Prior to World War II, the arrangements for employing basic science faculty in most of the medical schools in the United States were very different from the arrangements for employing their clinical faculty. Basic scientists were generally employed under terms similar to those for other university faculty members; they were considered full-time employees of their university (or their college in the few free standing medical schools). They were subject to the same or similar provisions for earning tenure, promotion, benefits and retirement that applied to all other faculty although they were more frequently on 12 month rather than nine or ten month contracts. In contrast, at most medical schools, a majority of the clinical faculty members were independent practicing physicians who either contracted to devote a specified amount of time to teaching, or in some instances contributed teaching time in exchange for the prestige associated with a clinical professorial title. Generally, medical schools awarded only one professorship in each clinical specialty; this to the department head or chairman who might, but might not be a full time employee. Such arrangements for clinical faculty depended heavily on the individual physician's motivation to be a teacher, be of service, be stimulated by contacts with students, or enjoy the recognition that was associated with faculty status. Since, at that time, much medical education took place in community hospitals where teaching patients were generally drawn from the uninsured and medically indigent, the disposition of fees for the professional services of the clinical faculty was not a major issue.

Following World War II there was a movement in medical education toward university hospitals and the development of full time clinical faculties, at least in such key departments as medicine, surgery and pediatrics. In order to pay for this, schools began to broaden the base of "teaching patients" to include those able to pay for their services. This was justified by the realization that medical students would benefit from exposure to a broader spectrum of patients and complaints. A variety of so-called "practice plans" were developed in order to incorporate patients' fees into compensation for clinical faculty.

As an example of this trend, when Bill Willard arrived at the medical school in Syracuse in 1950, the Department of Medicine was the only clinical department with full time faculty members - just a chairman and seven others. In the other departments, even the chairmen were only part time employees of the school and were maintaining their private practices in the community. Part of his mandate for upgrading the school was the development of full time clinical departments; an undertaking that had been virtually completed when he left Syracuse for Lexington six years later.

In the transition from voluntary or part time to full time clinical faculties, medical schools developed a variety of salary plans for physicians. One type of arrangement became known as the "full full-time" plan. First developed at Yale, "full full-time" implied that the physician faculty members' full salaries would be paid by the College in return for their devoting full time to teaching, research, teaching-related patient care, and other activities such as committee assignments that were in support of the medical school's education and research mission. The only exceptions might be compensation for non-recurring professional activities such as providing a guest lecture or providing a non-patient care related consultation. In support of full full-time was the assumption that only by providing full compensation could medical schools expect their physician faculty members to devote their total attention to the teaching, research, and service missions of a medical school. The major argument against a full full-time arrangement was from some physicians who felt they should have the right to and should insist on maintaining control over the disposition of funds that were generated as fees for their professional services. Such a position was supported by the American Medical Association that also opposed what they called the "corporate practice of medicine." Also, some medical schools felt that they simply could not afford a full full-time arrangement.

Between the concept of full full-time and the no longer acceptable reliance on part time and voluntary faculties, many medical schools adopted what became known simply as "full time" plans. Although there were as many variations as there were plans, the essence of a full time plan is that faculty members are considered full time employees of their medical schools but all or part of their salaries are derived from fees generated by their professional services and the distribution of these fees is determined by the faculty themselves. Such plans generally provide for some portion of the fees to be assigned to the medical school to pay for facilities and supportive personnel, but ultimate control of the funds from physician fees for service is retained by the physicians.

At the University of Kentucky, one of the planning tasks was to visit medical schools where various physician practice plans had been adopted and to evaluate their advantages and disadvantages. This review provided strong support for a full full-time plan. Such a plan was consistent with the philosophical goal of encouraging collaboration between basic science and clinical faculty members in education and research and collaboration among the clinical specialists in providing comprehensive patient care. It was seen as protecting the availability of physicians to participate fully in the non-income generating activities of the school. And, it was seen as providing a distinct advantage in the recruitment of physician faculty members who would be fully committed to their roles as educators and investigators and not feel compelled to "earn their own salaries." Kentucky established what was called the Physician's Services Plan (PSP). This initial plan provided for physicians to be in tenured or tenure track faculty positions and for their salaries to be determined by the same types of criteria as those of other University faculty members. Physicians were not involved in the billing, collecting or disposition of fees for services. Fees were deposited in a Fund for the Advancement of Medical Education and Research (that also served as a depository for overhead from research and training grants) and were used to support the academic programs of the College. A faculty advisory committee to the PSP included basic science as well as clinical members.

For the College of Medicine at that time, the PSP concept had many advantages. In the late 1950s there was a distinct trend toward full full-time practice plans for physicians in American medical schools. This trend was encouraged by the Association of American Medical Colleges. It was an attractive plan for physicians who wanted to teach or do research for it offered them a secure income without all of the hassle and uncertainty associated with private practice. It also permitted the medical school to be competitive with private practice in attracting faculty. At that time a professor of medicine who might be a department chairman would probably be paid between 20 and 25 thousand dollars, depending on the school. The same individual, as a highly respected practicing physician, might expect to clear between 30 and 35 thousand dollars from a private practice, depending on the community. For most aspiring academic physicians at that time the difference in potential income was a price they expected to pay for the advantages of academic medicine. At Kentucky, although conditions were to change rapidly in the 1960s, the full full-time plan was initially a distinct asset in the recruitment of physician faculty members who were attracted by and committed to the philosophical goals of the school and who welcomed the opportunity to become fully involved in the development of educational and patient care programs without worrying about generating their own income directly from patient fees. Conversely, those who rejected the PSP concept were apt also to find incompatibility with philosophical and educational goals of the College.

The PSP was an important factor in easing the concerns and potential opposition of community physicians and hospitals where there was potential tension around feared competition for patients. Because the College of Medicine's income from fees could be seen as a byproduct of education and as essential to the support of education, potential conflicts regarding competition were moderated.

Within the College, the PSP concept had an equalizing effect. It minimized awareness of the differences in the income raising potentiality of the various medical specialties and between physicians and basic scientists. It lent support to a sense of faculty solidarity in which all were equally involved in pursuing the educational, research, service and philosophical goals of the College. Although designed to meet very practical ends, the PSP as it evolved was still one more expression of the Statement of Philosophy of Medical Education that guided the planning and development of the College.

THE MEDICAL LIBRARY

Recognition of the importance of a medical library as an essential component of a college of medicine was included in the several studies and reports that led up to the establishment of the College and the Medical Center. Because of the time required to search for, acquire and organize the collections of basic journals and books that would be needed as the core of a Library, Dr. Willard gave the recruitment of a head medical librarian and the allocation of funds for a library a high priority. Because architectural planning was already in progress, immediate attention also had to be given to the location and design of a library facility within the medical center complex. The architects were asked to provide for the library a central location, ample space, and the potential for accommodating a substantial expansion of the library's collections and increase in the number of its users.

A national search for the medical librarian resulted in the recruitment of Alfred N. Brandon. Although he was appointed in July 1957, Al Brandon had a prior commitment to fulfill, and was forced to commute from California for about three months before he could move his family and transfer his full-time effort to Lexington. This did not deter him from hiring some staff and "starting" his library. Brandon was a librarian who believed that his function was to circulate, not just collect and protect a library's holdings. Within days after he initially arrived in Lexington with his stationwagon full of books and journals that he had collected in California and along the way, Al made it possible for interested persons to borrow these items. For the next several years, although the Library's collections were expanding rapidly and had to be stored in remote places, they were made available for circulation almost as fast as they were acquired.

The Medical Library provided an early opportunity for concrete collaboration between the Medical Center and the

University at large. Organizationally, it was agreed that the Medical Library would be considered a unit of the University Library System as well as the Medical Center. All materials in the Medical Library would be represented in the University Library catalog. At the same time, the Director of Libraries, Lawrence Thompson, a classics scholar, respected the specialized nature of a medical library and Alfred Brandon was accorded relative autonomy to pursue his task.

In 1918, after University President Frank L. McVey had first seriously explored the possibility of starting a College of Medicine, the University's Library had begun subscribing to some medical journals and collecting other medically relevant items. It was now agreed that these materials would be transferred to the Medical Library and, thus, would not have to be duplicated. The University's King Library that had housed the Medical Center's planning staff on a temporary basis, also provided initial working space for Mr. Brandon and his staff and storage space for some of the medical collections.

It quickly became clear that Al Brandon knew what to look for, where to find it and how to acquire it. Within a short time he was able to locate duplicate holdings in other libraries and arrange to acquire them. Some were gifts. Others he negotiated to purchase. Soon he was acquiring some duplicates of his own and arranging to exchange these for items he lacked. Colleagues on the planning staff and in the University Library watched in amazement as Brandon performed what became known as his "hat tricks."

The Library became the Medical Center's first major beneficiary of significant gifts. With substantial assistance from William Arnold Hanger, the Library acquired a 4,300 volume collection of journals from the Wistar Institute of Anatomy and Physiology in Philadelphia. The National Library of Medicine donated 16 cartons of medical journals plus indexes to medical literature, past and present. Several of Kentucky's physicians contributed valuable books, old instruments and other important artifacts.

All told, by the time that the Medical Library was formally dedicated, coincidental with the arrival of students in the fall of 1960, its collection of 50,000 volumes exceeded by 20,000 the goal that had been set in early 1958. In addition, it was subscribing to 1,200 journals and other serials. (A year later there would be nearly 70,000 volumes and more than 1,500 serials.) Speaking at the Library's formal dedication in 1960, Robert T. Lentz, president of the National Medical Library Association, noted that the Library had already reached the median figure for number of volumes held by medical libraries throughout the country and contained more volumes than the libraries of several long established medical schools in the region. Referring to the brief period allowed for acquiring these collections, Lentz said that "anyone in the medical library field" if "told to meet such a quota, would have said it was impossible."

TAKING TIME OUT TO LOOK TOWARD THE FUTURE

By September 1958, two years into the planning and development process, planning for the physical plant was essentially completed and construction of the Medical Center's basic facilities was well under way. The next major tasks were to be the recruitment of a faculty and staff, the detailed development of a curriculum for the College and more refined preparation for research and patient care activities.

At this point, the staff took time to look beyond their immediate tasks and pressures in order to consider the long range development of the Medical Center. A staff memorandum dated September 10, 1958 entitled "An Approach to the Future Development of the University of Kentucky Medical Center" was submitted to and "approved" by President Dickey and the Board of Trustees. This document reiterated the major purposes for which the Medical Center had been established — to provide more doctors and health personnel for Kentucky, especially in underserved areas of the State; to provide more opportunities for Kentucky's youth to prepare for careers in the health professions; and to improve the level of health and the quality of and access to health care for Kentucky's people. It restated basic philosophical objectives and it stressed the importance of obtaining adequate operating funds for the College and the Center and the need eventually to expand the 39 acre site designated for the Medical Center.

The memorandum then related the mission and goals of the Center to a need for support for programs and facilities that were not provided or projected at that time. These included scholarships, loan funds and fellowships for students; an "emergency fund" to meet unanticipated requirements; funds for library enrichment, special lectureships, and extensive postgraduate education and in-service training programs; funds to provide an endowment of academic chairs or departments; and support for programs that would focus on a number of special needs for which resources in Kentucky were underdeveloped. These needs included chronic diseases, rehabilitation, mental health, aging, maternal and child health, occupational health, and the fields of medical economics, medical sociology and medical administration. Facilities recommended for the future included a center for continuing education, student dormitories, expanded research facilities, rural teaching and research centers, a child study center, and a rehabilitation dormitory and nursing home that would permit extensions of the hospital's services.

In order to finance these recommendations for the future, the memorandum suggested that a program for private fund raising be developed, "aimed at providing that margin of supplementary support required for the quality and level and vitality of program development requisite to a great medical center—one which will be equal to challenges ahead and able to capitalize on the opportunities presented."

Although these recommendations may have seemed grandiose to some, they were consistent with the goals of quality medical education and with the frequently identified special needs of Kentucky. Furthermore, when they were being recruited, Dr. Willard and his staff had been encouraged by the members of the Kentucky Medical Foundation and others to expect a significant amount of private financial support for the Medical Center. With a few exceptions, despite the Foundations' valiant effort, such support was not forthcoming at that time. Much of Lexington's wealth was represented in families who had homes in several locations and were directing their philanthropy elsewhere. In addition, most wealthy Lexingtonians, including most members of the medical profession, did not have a record of generous giving to their community. The University at that time did not have either a tradition or a mechanism for seeking significant private funds. As will be seen, many of the 1958 recommendations for "future development" were eventually implemented even though, when originally formulated, they were somewhat ahead of their time.

HELP FROM THE PRIVATE SECTOR

Although early efforts to attract significant contributions from the private sector fell far short of aspirations, there were still several successes. The Commonwealth Fund of New York City guided by its Executive Director, Lester J. Evans, had developed a special interest in innovations in medical education. Dr. Evans was one of the consultants who had recommended Bill Willard to the University of Kentucky. In March, 1957 the Commonwealth Fund provided a grant of $73,400 to help support planning activities especially as they related to meeting the special needs of Kentucky's people. With some of these funds, Thomas R. Ford, a demographer on the U.K. faculty in sociology and rural sociology, was recruited to join the staff on a half time basis for two years in order to conduct a study of demography and health in Kentucky. Ford's findings replaced what had previously been merely impressions about the health status of Kentuckians. Subsequently revised to reflect 1960 census data, the study was published in book form. (Thomas R. Ford, *Health and Demography in Kentucky*, Lexington: University of Kentucky Press, 1964.) Another sociologist, John H. Mabry, was also recruited under the Commonwealth Fund grant to conduct a series of studies on patterns of response to illness among Kentucky's people. The findings of this work were later reflected in both the curriculum and in provisions for patient care. Additionally, the Commonwealth grant supported much of the travel that permitted members of the planning staff to visit other medical centers, seeking suggestions, testing ideas and beginning to scout for promising faculty members.

In September 1957, it was learned that the College of Medicine had been named as a beneficiary in the will of Elise Shackleford, former owner of the *Thoroughbred Record*. This was welcome news and raised the hope that others would emulate Ms. Shackleford.

In August 1959, the University received an unusually restricted gift from Mr. Will Clayton of Texas. Mr. Clayton, a wealthy farm owner and authority on world trade, had maintained a summer home called Cave Hill in the southwestern section of Lexington. As an expression of his interest in and support for the Medical Center he gave Cave Hill and its surrounding acreage to the University with the stipulation that it be used as a home for the Dean of the College of Medicine. Unfortunately, there was no way that Dr. Willard, on his relatively modest salary, could afford to live in or maintain the Cave Hill estate, nor was the home's isolated location suitable to the needs of the Willard household. Because negotiations designed to modify the restriction were unsuccessful, the University was unable to benefit from the gift. (The Cave Hill mansion and estate later became the Lexington home of Governor John Y. Brown and his wife Phyllis George.)

THE RECRUITMENT PROCESS

With the building program underway, the next major step in the development of the College of Medicine was the recruitment of department chairs. The goal was to have chairmen on hand well before the activation of their programs so that they could participate in the development of the curriculum and the patient care program and could have ample time to recruit the members of their own departments. Of first priority was the recruitment of chairmen for the departments that would be involved in the first year curriculum. These included the traditional subjects of anatomy, physiology and biochemistry. In addition, in accordance with the College's philosophical objectives there would be first year teaching responsibilities for the behavioral sciences and for the clinical departments of medicine, pediatrics and psychiatry. (Considerations leading to a decision to have a department of behavioral science will be discussed below.)

In the 1950s, the identification of potential faculty members was conducted largely by word of mouth. Deans and chairmen were notified of vacancies and asked to recommend potential candidates from among their own faculty or former students or others whom they knew. Positions were rarely advertised. This was particularly the case with colleges of medicine.

At Kentucky the search process really began with visits to other medical schools to look at architectural arrangements and seek suggestions about things that should be done "differently." During these visits, there were also opportunities to discuss the Kentucky philosophy and to "scout" for suggestions about promising faculty with a potential for leadership and a motivation for experimentation. As suggestions were collected and reviewed, Dr. Willard and other staff members began to visit potential candidates on their own campuses whenever their travel schedules permitted. Such visits afforded an opportunity to see the individuals in action and sometimes to judge how they related to their own colleagues. Also, on such occasions, the statement of philosophy of medical education and other planning documents were provided and reactions to these were invited. When a particularly attractive candidate was identified by one of the staff, another would be assigned to drop by for a second opinion. In this way, from fairly long lists of suggestions (as many as 60 for some positions), a relatively small number of attractive potential candidates were identified. The next step was to invite those who were interested to visit Lexington. The formula that Dr. Willard developed for these visits involved inviting two individuals from different disciplines to come at the same time for two or three day visits. During these visits the candidates usually spent time with the members of the planning staff, with President Dickey and selected faculty members and administrators of the University at large, and with some community physicians. Every meal was a working session and at least one evening was devoted to an open discussion of philosophical issues and more practical questions. Such sessions often went past midnight. Because funds for "professional entertainment" were not available, wives of the planning staff took turns sometimes providing "bed and breakfast" and often hosting the dinners and evening sessions all of which took place in their private homes.

When staff consensus was reached, Dr. Willard generally made another personal visit to the candidate of choice to check out any further questions and tender an invitation from the College. This process of search, selection and recruitment was so time consuming and demanding that it seldom could be followed after the activation of the College. However, it resulted in the recruitment of a cadre of young medical educators who helped lead the College of Medicine to its next stage of development. As testimony to Willard's gift for identifying the future potential in relatively young, often untested, individuals, many of those who he recruited in 1958 and 1959 became part of the next generation of medical education statesmen and it will be seen later that several went on to lead the development of new medical schools elsewhere.

In the early years of recruitment, it was not just potential chairmen who were offered personal hospitality and subjected to involved discussions of philosophical issues. Jacqueline Noonan, who was recruited by Jack Githens in 1961 as an Assistant Professor of Pediatrics, remembers being very impressed by the recruitment process. She was invited to stay in the Githens home, treated as a member of their family, and interviewed by Dean Willard and Drs. Pellegrino, Deuschle, Schwert, Carlson, and Straus, all department chairmen. She also participated in group discussions of philosophical as well as medical issues. Jackie (who later would herself chair the Department of Pediatrics) said that she felt "very special" and very excited when invited to come to Kentucky. "When I came everybody knew everyone else, not just in pediatrics but on the whole faculty." She may have been one of the last recruits to experience this process. By the early 1960s there were pressures for a much more rapid and less deliberate and selective process of faculty recruitment and the selection process tended to be restricted to within each department.

The intent of this history is to deal more with events than with personalities except where personalities clearly shaped events. Among these exceptions were three chairmen who were recruited in 1958 and arrived at the College in 1959 in time to join the planning staff and participate in the development of the initial curriculum and the selection of the first class of students and to begin considering program objectives for patient care. These were William H. Knisely, Anatomy; George W. Schwert, Biochemistry; and Edmund D. Pellegrino, Internal Medicine. Sometime later they were joined by Joseph B. Parker, Psychiatry and Loren D. Carlson, Physiology. Their contributions to the College's formative history will be discussed in later sections.

A BETTER MOUSETRAP

As the buildings of the Medical Center began to rise above the ground its relative immensity in comparison with all of the other facilities that were then on the University campus became apparent. It also became common knowledge that the Center would be air-conditioned, a "luxury" undreamed of by most other university faculty and students, and that the spaces allotted for the library, laboratories, offices and teaching areas would appear to be large and luxurious in contrast to the overcrowded firetraps in which some of the University was forced to function. For some of those persons who had feared the Medical Center's impact, its appearance in concrete reality reinforced their convictions that all hope for upgrading the University at large was now lost. Increasingly, however, members of the University family began to look on the Medical Center as what Allen M. Trout of the Louisville *Courier-Journal* (borrowing from Emerson) called a "Better Mousetrap." Citing a self-study report from the University, Trout wrote that the Medical Center "has stimulated the rest of the university to reach for betterment" and "is the catalytic agent that (has) triggered constructive unrest on the academic campus." The self-study recommendations called for upgrading salaries, facilities and other university resources to match those of the Medical Center. Trout concluded "the faculty reacted with wisdom that, in the end, will probably prevail because it is unassailable. This wise decision is not to try to tear the Medical Center down, but to try to build arts and sciences up to it." (Louisville *Courier-Journal*, May 1, 1960). Events of the 1960s would prove that Trout was a good prophet.

DEPARTMENTAL UNITY

As planning for the College of Medicine went forward there was a continuing area of tension over the University's policy of "departmental unity" which held that no subject could be taught by more than one department. This raised the expectations of some faculty that existing Departments in the College of Arts and Sciences such as Bacteriology, Anatomy and Physiology, Psychology, and Public Health would be responsible for teaching their subjects in the College of Medicine. However, there were major differences in experience, orientation and philosophy between the programs of these departments and the curriculum that was being developed for the College of Medicine. Potential problems were easily resolved in three of these areas. The Psychology Department modified its "claim" with respect to Psychiatry. The faculty members in Public Health had been actively involved in the University's Health Service and their positions were transferred with the Health Service to the Medical Center. Loren D. Carlson who was recruited to chair the College of Medicine's Department of Physiology invited the four faculty members of Anatomy and Physiology to transfer from the College of Arts and Science to the College of Medicine where they continued to be active in undergraduate and graduate teaching while developing useful new roles in the medical curriculum and enjoying expanded research facilities. Unfortunately, an acceptable resolution of the primacy issue was not found in the case of Bacteriology. Dr. Morris Scherago, the Chairman of Bacteriology was a veterinarian by profession. He insisted that his department was fully qualified to teach microbiology to medical students. He successfully petitioned the University Faculty, chaired by his departmental colleague, Dr. Ralph Weaver, to approve a change in the name of his department from Bacteriology to Microbiology and then claimed that no microbiology could be taught in the University outside of his department. Scherago had prepared his ground well. He and Weaver were astute practitioners of university politics. They became champions of those who were negative or ambivalent about the impact of the medical school on the University or who were attracted to the idea that someone was standing up to the giant. Rather than cause a major issue or risk losing some of the support it had gained, the medical school withdrew its plans for a Department of Microbiology. For several years, while Drs. Scherago and Weaver held reign, this component of the medical curriculum was provided by faculty from other departments of the College of Medicine.

Because, in keeping with Bill Willard's convictions that physicians should be exposed to the social and behavioral sciences, subjects such as sociology, anthropology and psychology were to be included in the medical curriculum, these were also areas of potential jurisdictional dispute. Problems never developed, largely because a pattern of collaboration and joint appointments was established with the Department of Sociology when the planning staff first arrived and was later adopted by other social and behavioral science departments.

A PLACE FOR BEHAVIORAL SCIENCE

As the planning process moved toward 1959, a number of organizational questions had already been resolved. The Medical Center had been established as a major sector of the University with its own Vice President who reported to the President and the Board of Trustees. Under the Vice President for the Medical Center, three Colleges - Medicine, Dentistry and Nursing - had been established, each with its own Dean. Other units of the Medical Center included the University Hospital, the Medical Library, and the University Health Service, each with its own Director.

As already mentioned, considerable thought had been given to organizing the College of Medicine without traditional departments, but, in the interest of faculty recruitment, the departmental structure had been retained. However, in keeping with the philosophical goal of fostering a health team concept by developing some shared educational experiences for students of the various health professions, it was intended that the basic science departments of the College of Medicine would be responsible for providing instruction for students of dentistry, nursing and other programs for health professionals that might be developed.

Early in his discussions about a move to Kentucky, Dr. Willard made clear his convictions about the relevance of the social and behavioral sciences to medical education and medical practice. He made sure that a behavioral science perspective was significantly conspicuous in the planning process. During the 1950s, Willard's pioneer introduction of behavioral science concepts and content into the medical curriculum had been emulated by a number of other medical schools. In 1957, the Council on Medical Education and Hospitals of the American Medical Association revised its "essentials of an acceptable medical school" to add "human behavior" to its list of subjects required as "basic knowledge" in medical education. However, no common organizational pattern had emerged. In several schools, one or more behavioral scientists worked out of the Dean's office, giving lectures or seminars here and there as they might be invited to participate or be interposed on various courses. Some schools followed the model Dr. Willard had used at SUNY Syracuse by appointing behavioral scientist(s) in Departments of Public Health and/or Preventive Medicine. The most common pattern that emerged during the 1950s was to add behavioral science position(s) to Departments of Psychiatry. Observations of these various patterns revealed that the roles and contributions of behavioral scientists were generally limited to participation in the primary missions of their particular department or unit.

None of these arrangements were compatible with the basic conviction at Kentucky that the theories, content and methods of the social and behavioral sciences were basic to all of medical practice - not just to psychiatry or prevention or public health - and basic to the other health professions as well. In addition, it had been found in the planning process, that a behavioral science perspective could be relevant to decisions ranging from faculty recruitment and student selection to curriculum design and provisions for patient care. These considerations led to a decision to recommend to the Board of Trustees the establishment of the first Department of Behavioral Science in a college of medicine. This would be a basic science department whose faculty would be responsible for teaching in each college of the Medical Center and for research that would be particularly relevant to the goals of health care. Following a precedent established with the Department of Sociology, graduate courses in the medical behavioral sciences would be offered for students enrolled in existing graduate programs on the main campus.

The decision to create a Department of Behavioral Science was strongly influenced by organizational theory. Departmental status and structure was seen as the best way to assure acceptance for and the inclusion of the behavioral sciences and behavioral scientists, not just in the curriculum, but in the overall decision-making process and power structure of the College.

On February 20, 1959 the University Board of Trustees approved the establishment of a Department of Behavioral Science in the College of Medicine. The proposal for the Department that was presented to the Board included the following statement: "The basic objectives and orientation of the University of Kentucky Medical Center require the development of substantial strength in the area of behavioral science. The Center is committed to a philosophy of comprehensive patient care and to programs of education and research based on the concepts of comprehensive medicine. Comprehensive medicine involves the organization of health resources to deal with the total health of a patient through an integrated, continuing plan incorporating prevention, rehabilitation, and long-term care, as well as diagnosis and treatment of specific symptoms. The comprehensive approach to health care calls for consideration of the interaction in human behavior of psychological, social, and cultural factors with biological and physical factors. The behavioral sciences provide both a theoretical framework and research findings that give added validity, depth and significance to the overall understanding of causes, prevalence, course, and clinical management of patients' health problems, their impact on family, job, and community situations, social structure, and interaction in the therapeutic setting. The University of Kentucky Medical Center is committed to the health team concept....Behavioral Science research is basic to the understanding of role relationships between various members of the health team."

Once its establishment was approved, the Department of Behavioral Science rapidly took shape. From the original planning staff, Alan Ross elected to join the department. Ross's decision meant that the Department of Behavioral Science would benefit from his statistical orientation and would assume the additional roles of teaching statistics to medical students and providing consultation for the faculty of the College on research design and data analysis. Some of the personnel who were working on studies supported by the Commonwealth Fund grant also joined the Department giving it a head start on recruitment.

With the establishment of the Department of Behavioral Science, I became its first Chairman, a role I would fill for 28 years. Despite his strong support for the department, Dr. Willard was actually quite ambivalent about this appointment. As members of the planning group in Kentucky began to specialize, my responsibilities were increasingly concerned with architectural features related to the learning process, curriculum design, scouting for potential faculty, and educational aspects of patient care. As a logical transition, Dr. Willard wanted to create for me a position as Associate Dean and Assistant Vice President for Academic Affairs. Sensing that my own strengths and personal comfort lay more in teaching and research than in administration, I was reluctant to assume these responsibilities and give up the opportunity offered by the Department of Behavioral Science. We finally agreed that I would carry the academic affairs roles on a "part time" basis during the period of transition to full activation. (This turned out to be three years.) However, I chose a less formal and imposing title of Coordinator of Academic Affairs (for both the College and the Medical Center).

The responsibilities of the Coordinator as designated by Dr. Willard in a memo of March 15, 1960 were appallingly broad, something like the duties of Gilbert and Sullivan's "Lord-high everything else:": "(1) curriculum and the academic schedule, (2) admissions, (3) student affairs, (4) academic evaluation and (5) special projects as these may be assigned." However, it was understood that as activation and growth of the college and the Medical Center justified the hiring of more personnel the direct responsibility for these duties would be transferred to others. A major step in this direction was the appointment of Roy Jarecky in July 1961 to handle admissions and student affairs. At that point the academic folders of our first 40 students were transferred from my desk drawer to Roy's.

I was concerned lest my dean type roles would conflict with developing a comfortable give and take with the other department chairs. I asked them directly how they felt about this. Bill Knisely said "Bob, as long as you don't get to enjoy functioning like a dean, it will be O.K., but if you enjoy it, we'll give you a hard time." I never did enjoy it.

SOME UNCOMMON RECRUITING

Just as Bill Willard had "raised eyebrows" when he included three non-physicians on his initial four member planning staff, he continued to surprise traditionalists in the medical profession and the University with many of his selections for department chairs and key administrative positions. Many were quite young or they had not risen through the usual progression of academic ranks. Alan Ross was 30 when he joined the planning staff, Dick Wittrup just 31 when he was selected to become the hospital administrator, Noback and Straus were just 33. Bill Knisely was 36. Later Peter Bosomworth would be appointed chairman of Anesthesiology at the age of 32, Harold Rosenbaum as chairman of Radiology at age 34 and Jack Green as chairman of Obstetrics and Gynecology at age 36.

There was no better example of Willard's disregard for the orthodox than the selection of Edmund D. Pellegrino to be the chairman of the Department of Internal Medicine. As soon as he accepted the job in Lexington, Willard began to hear from Lester Evans, President of the Commonwealth Fund, about Ed Pellegrino. Evans was a strong advocate of medical education innovation. He had helped persuade Willard to come to Kentucky, provided a grant to help in the planning process and visited Lexington on several occasions. Evans and the Commonwealth Fund were also supporting an innovative program of medical education that New York University's medical school had established at the Hunterton Medical Center in rural Flemington, New Jersey. Pellegrino was medical director and director of internal medicine at Hunterton and held a faculty appointment at N.Y.U. Under Pellegrino's direction, Hunterton was providing a unique link between academic medicine, a community hospital and the practicing physicians of a primarily rural area. As a teaching hospital for N.Y.U. it was providing community physicians with the opportunity to admit their private patients and retain responsibility for their care while they and their patients could benefit from consultation with and supervision of clinical faculty from N.Y.U. It was a unique marriage between academic and community based medicine and an experiment that Lester Evans thought could have important implications for Kentucky. Edmund Pellegrino had been one of the architects of the Hunterton plan as well as its chief medical officer.

One by one, Willard and other members of the planning staff made an opportunity to visit Hunterton and meet Pellegrino. They sensed that many aspects of the Hunterton philosophy and plan were compatible with their goals for Kentucky and they saw in Ed Pellegrino a man of impressive intellectual stature, medical competence and social conscience. Ed Pellegrino was a true Renaissance man; a scholar of philosophy and ancient cultures, an ethicist, a superb medical diagnostician and teacher and a man of compassion. When Pellegrino visited Lexington, key faculty members and administrators throughout the University and members of the local medical community were equally impressed. However, because Pellegrino had not yet progressed through the traditional academic ranks nor yet produced the mass of traditionally expected research papers in referred scientific journals, it is doubtful that he would have been considered at that time for the position of chairman of medicine at any of the established medical schools in the country. This did not faze Bill Willard who saw in Ed Pellegrino just the man to help Kentucky's College of Medicine meet its unique objectives. In the Fall of 1958 Pellegrino was offered and accepted an appointment as Professor and Chairman of Medicine. When he arrived a few months later, Ed Pellegrino immediately became a dynamic contributor to the planning process. He helped design the initial curriculum, was a respected ambassador to the health professions, and he chaired the committee that was formed to develop guidelines and specific plans for the programs of patient care in the University Hospital. (After spending eight years at Kentucky, Ed Pellegrino would be recruited to develop and direct the State University of New York's new Health Sciences Center at Stony Brook and be the Dean of its School of Medicine. He would subsequently become Chancellor for the University of Tennessee's medical units in Memphis, serve as President of the Yale-New Haven Medical Center, become President of the Catholic University of America, and finally assume several roles in medicine, philosophy, ethics and the medical humanities at Georgetown University.)

Another unlikely choice was that of Joseph Parker to head the Department of Psychiatry. Parker's primary interests were in community psychiatry. In this he was nearly a decade ahead of most of his profession. He also expressed comfort with the proposed concept of teaching much of clinical psychiatry within the context of comprehensive medicine. And at a time when many academic psychiatrists were beginning to claim the behavioral sciences as their territory, Parker expressed support for a separate (basic science) department and for the concept that the behavioral sciences had potential application to all of the fields of medicine. For these reasons, although Parker was not then on anyone else's list of potential department chairmen, he was considered well suited to develop a department at Kentucky. Joe Parker's relative comfort with respect to our behavioral science arrangement was shaken a bit when he received a note from the Chairman of Psychiatry at the University of Louisville, welcoming him to the State and asking if he would "be in Bob Straus's department."

Still another example of Bill Willard's recruiting that defied convention was the selection of Kurt Deuschle in 1960 to chair the Department of Community Medicine. Writing about this in 1972, Deuschle recalled "He (Willard) took considerable risk to bring an assistant professor from Cornell to Lexington and give him a chairmanship of the 'first' department of Community Medicine. It was through his vision, insight, and warm endorsement that I found the resources for developing a viable and significant experiment in medical education." A consideration of the concept and the unique contributions of Deuschle's Community Medicine Department will be included in Chapter Six.

Harold Rosenbaum was the first Kentuckian to be recruited as a departman chairman. Harold was born and raised in a rural area about 100 miles south of Lexington. He was a graduate of Berea College and the Harvard Medical School and had returned to Kentucky and a private practice in radiology when he was invited by Dr. Willard to develop and chair the Department of Radiology. Harold's selection was applauded by the local medical community. In addition to his scholarship and scientific and clinical expertise, Harold brought to the College an understanding of Kentucky culture that would prove of great value in his contributions to both education and patient care.

For his administrative staff, Dr. Willard also made a number of appointments that were unusual for that time. In 1960 he created a staff position, eventually called Director of State and Local Services, with a major responsibility for extending the services and impact of the Medical Center and the College of Medicine beyond its walls. For this unique role he turned to the field of public health and recruited Robert L. Johnson. Also still in his 30's, Johnson brought professional maturity, interpersonal skills and a vision that enabled him to develop a unique program of outreach services extending to all regions of the State. One of Bob Johnson's more innovative approaches was to work with the extension agents in the College of Agriculture as both a model and a medium for service delivery. Bob Johnson's subsequent career justified the potential that Bill Willard saw in him. After a career of ever increasing responsibilities that included serving as Vice President of the University of California, Johnson eventually returned to Kentucky where as President of Appalachian Regional Healthcare he was instrumental in rescuing this critical non-profit source of health care for the people of Eastern Kentucky from the brink of bankruptcy and creating a viable and comprehensive program of health services.

Still one more example of Bill Willard's unorthodox recruiting and one that anticipated a trend, was his selection in 1961 of Roy K. Jarecky as Director of Student Services. This was at a time when comparable positions in other medical schools were traditionally filled by physicians, many of whom had become disillusioned by or disinterested in the practice of medicine and provided uninspiring role models for aspiring physicians. Roy Jarecky had a degree in student personnel administration from Columbia University's Teachers College. He brought to his job a concern for student development and well being that extended far beyond routine services and record keeping. He was encouraged by Bill Willard to acquire expertise in and develop a program of research in medical education. During what would be thirty years of service to the College in various capacities Roy would contribute to creativity in admissions, curriculum and administration. Always, he would be viewed as an advocate of diversity in student selection and of flexibility for the student experience.

Frank Dickey, in recalling some of Bill Willard's many accomplishments while he (Dickey) was President of the University of Kentucky has referred to Willard's "remarkable judgment in selecting individuals for the staff and faculty who had the potential to become real leaders in their own right." This would certainly seem to have included some of Willard's more unorthodox selections.

SELECTION AND ADMISSION OF STUDENTS

Even before Dr. Willard and his planning staff set up shop in Lexington, inquiries began to be made about how to apply for admission to the College of Medicine. On the day in the fall of 1956 that staff members first occupied their temporary space, two aspirants found their way to the bowels of the King Library to ask when and how they might apply. From then on, numerous unsolicited letters of recommendation were received on behalf of potential applicants.

This interest in the school was in part a reflection of the limited opportunities that then existed for qualified Kentuckians to attend a medical school. Although the University of Louisville's school had expanded its class size to and beyond the limit of its physical plant, it was heavily dependent on income from tuition and therefore was admitting a significant number of students from out-of-state, especially those whose academic qualifications were combined with an ability to pay full tuition. On the other hand, medical schools in nearby states, most of which were publicly supported, had for many years admitted only a token number of students from Kentucky. Thus, as the various studies that led up to the establishment of the school at U.K. had reported, there was a backlog of academically qualified Kentuckians who had sought and been denied the opportunity for a medical education and their numbers were increasing yearly.

Although there had been powerful forces in the Louisville community that had opposed the establishment of a medical school at the University of Kentucky, as already noted, Dean Murray Kinsman had not been one of them. Bill Willard and Murray Kinsman had served on committees together and come to respect each other. Dr. Willard was particularly hopeful that the Louisville school would not be harmed by the development in Lexington and that there would not be destructive competition. On a positive note, at the same time that the General Assembly made its initial appropriation for a medical center in Lexington, it had increased the level of State support for Louisville's medical school from $125,000 to $500,000 per year.

One area in which the schools would inevitably compete was for the best qualified Kentucky applicants. In order to make this process as constructive as possible, Drs. Kinsman and Willard agreed quite early to maintain open lines of communication and seek opportunities for collaboration around issues of admission. They decided to present a common front in the form of two jointly sponsored conferences on medical college admissions; the first was held in Lexington in March 1959, the second, in Louisville a year later. Invitations to these conferences were extended to all of the premedical advisors from Kentucky's undergraduate colleges and from selected schools in surrounding states. The conference that was held in Lexington attracted nearly 100 participants.

Themes stressed at the conference included the need for more flexibility in the premedical curriculum (by Dr. William J. Hockaday, director of admissions at Louisville); the opportunities for mutual assistance and cooperation (by Dean Kinsman of Louisville); the need to attract students motivated to meet the health needs of Kentuckians (by Dean Willard); the need for a significant portion of medical graduates to be prepared for family practice and the need of physicians to think of patients as people and as members of society (by Dr. Edmund D. Pellegrino, Chairman of the Department of Medicine at U.K.); the need for physicians to develop a spirit of inquiry and continue to grow and learn throughout their professional lives (by Robert Straus as chair of the U.K. admissions committee).

An unanticipated outcome of this conference was the initial racial integration of Lexington's then leading hotel, the Lafayette. When the conference was being planned, the question of segregation did not occur to those of us responsible for making the arrangements. (We were all from the northeast.) Although we had invited several blacks to the conference, it was only on the morning that conferees were due to register that we realized there could be a problem. The integration of public facilities was occurring gradually in Kentucky at that time and we were not aware that the Lafayette had made such a move. Rather than risk rejection, we decided not to raise the issue that morning, but to stand by and be prepared, if necessary, to offer the black conferees our apologies and the hospitality of our homes. Fortunately, when the black conferees arrived they were registered without question. We later learned that the hotel management had made the decision to integrate, but rather than risk any unpleasant demonstrations that might result from publicity about their decision, they were simply prepared to let their action speak instead of their words whenever the occasion should arise. It just so happened that our conference provided the initial opportunity for them to put their new policy into effect. That evening, at our conference dinner, the decision to integrate was reflected in the obvious pleasure expressed by several of the black waiters who, for the first time, served dinner to black guests.

Long before this conference, as an outgrowth of the statement on philosophy of medical education and in response to numerous inquiries, the planning staff had addressed the question of admission criteria. As with other planning issues, the admissions personnel of several other schools were asked about their own experiences and their suggestions for change, and the critical thinking of selected medical education leaders was solicited.

The suggestions we received, combined with our own philosophical objectives and concern for the special needs of Kentucky, all indicated that our admission criteria should include substantial flexibility. This was not characteristic of the admission requirements of most medical schools at that time.

A pamphlet entitled "How to Apply for Admission" was prepared for distribution to potential applicants. In keeping with the original 1956 statement of philosophy of medical education, the pamphlet promised an emphasis on "concepts of comprehensive medicine." It noted that program and facilities were "designed to provide opportunities for integrated instruction within and among the basic and clinical sciences." In addition to "a thorough grounding in the principles of each major scientific and clinical subject" the pamphlet promised a curriculum that would emphasize "the relationships between medical problems and total health; the role of emotional, social, and environmental factors in human response to illness and health needs; the importance of continuity in medical supervision and health maintenance; and opportunities for independent work in areas of special interest." It added "the school bears a special responsibility to prepare physicians who can meet the health needs of Kentucky, especially those in small towns and rural areas."

Preparation for admission to medical schools in the United States in the 1950s had become relatively standardized. Most aspirants were advised to major in chemistry, biology or physics or to take a "pre-medical" curriculum that was heavily loaded with the natural sciences. Although many of the medical schools suggested that applicants obtain a "liberal" undergraduate education, the majority of students that they selected were science or pre-med majors and, based on this, pre-med advisors (most of whom were chemists or biologists) continued to steer their physician aspirants away from courses in the humanities and social sciences. Students were advised that medical schools really didn't mean it when they advocated a liberal education. (Despite our efforts, and those of many other medical schools, to promote a liberal education as preparation for medical school many premedical advisors in the 1990s still tend to give contrary advice to aspiring medical students.)

In an effort to advise students responsibly so that they could qualify for admission to Kentucky and still be acceptable at other medical schools, the planning staff developed criteria for admission that emphasized balance. They established minimal requirements as the equivalent of "two semesters of study in physics; two semesters in the biological sciences; four semesters in chemistry, including organic chemistry; and at least one year of English with emphasis on communication skills such as reading, writing and speaking." Advanced work in mathematics and courses in the psychological and social sciences were "highly recommended." Students were also "encouraged to follow special interests which they may have in philosophy, literature or the fine arts." It was further suggested that "the student should demonstrate his capacity for advanced work through the concentrated study of at least one subject in a major area of his interest by completing courses beyond the introductory level which provide an opportunity for independent work." In order to further discourage students from following a "pre-med major" it was noted that "subjects such as human anatomy, medical biochemistry, medical bacteriology and mammalian physiology will be covered in medical school, and are not essential in premedical education." Candidates were advised that if they met the basic admission requirements and demonstrated excellence they would be given equal consideration whether they majored "in one of the natural sciences, the social sciences or in the humanities."

While the criteria of selection promised a preference for qualified residents of Kentucky, there were initially no legally mandated constraints on the admission of out-of-state candidates and it was felt that the inclusion of a few well qualified students from other parts of the country would enhance the educational experience of Kentuckians. In addition to measures of academic performance and aptitude (as measured by course grades and the Medical Collage Admission Test), emphasis was placed on "the communication skills demonstrated by each applicant. ... Communication is a two-way process and involves the ability to listen perceptively, as well as to speak and write clearly." It was noted also that "friendliness, warmth, compassion and integrity are all essential traits in the physician. The practice of medicine involves the physician in continual relationships with people— with his patients, and with other members of the health team. Often the physician's ability to communicate effectively will determine his degree of success in diagnosis and management of a patient's health problem and in his other professional activities." Finally, because of the demands of both medical education and medical practice on the individual, it was noted that "it is essential that a prospective medical student be in good health and that his motivation to study medicine be sufficiently strong to sustain him in the face of difficulties."

Although the admission pamphlet was addressed to the male gender, reflecting prevailing custom at that time and the fact that most physicians and medical students were then men, it was fully expected that women would apply and be admitted at the University of Kentucky. In fact, with this objective in mind, the architects had to modify their original plans in order to provide

119

adequate appropriate rest room facilities for women students.

Another policy in effect at the University at that time was to omit any reference to race on the application form. It was reasoned that the best way to assure equal opportunity based strictly on qualifications was to make the selection of candidates "blind" with respect to race. Of course, because the medical school admission process included personal interviews the "blind" choice applied only to the initial screening.

Although the College of Medicine was being designed to accommodate 75 medical students in each class, initial plans called for admitting only 30 to the first class and to increase the number admitted gradually to the full complement of 75. However, within a few months of planning, it became apparent that the original target date of Sept. 1959 for opening the school was too ambitious. The processes of design, bidding, awarding a contract, construction, recruiting a faculty and activation of facilities could not be completed within this time frame. Instead, the opening was deferred until 1960, but the number of students to be admitted to the first class was increased to 40. Applications for admission in September 1960 were to be accepted after July 1, 1959 with a deadline of February 1, 1960.

Many of the potential applicants who began making inquiries as early as September 1956 never actually applied. Some were able to attend the University of Louisville or another medical school. Some selected an alternative health profession. Some were forced by age or family responsibilities to seek other careers. Some just decided that medical school was "not in the cards" for them.

Nevertheless, when the dust had cleared, there were more than 400 applications for admission. Following a process followed by most medical schools, applications were initially reviewed by members of an admissions committee and divided into three groups on the basis of information contained on the application form, letters of reference, scores on the Medical College Admissions Test, and the applicants own "presentation of self" in essay form. The initial groups were "probably well qualified," "clearly unqualified" and "status unclear." All applicants but those clearly unqualified were to be offered opportunities for personal interviews. A "high powered" admissions committee for the first class consisted of five department chairmen (Pellegrino, Medicine; Knisely, Anatomy; Schwert, Biochemistry; Parker, Psychiatry; and Straus, Behavioral Science).

Although the new chairmen were busy recruiting faculty and staff for their own departments, ordering equipment, setting up their research, participating in curriculum development, and sharing some of the other tasks of activation, they all looked on the process of selecting students for the first class as a welcome challenge and opportunity. There was an opportunity to select some non traditional applicants including intellectually qualified students who did not have the usual background in the natural sciences. There was an intention that the class would include women and minorities. And there was a commitment to provide opportunities for qualified Kentuckians, especially those who hopefully would eventually practice medicine in underserved parts of the State. At the same time there was a realization that some of the applicants with the best qualifications would have an opportunity to go elsewhere. For these students, the admissions process including persuading them that the advantages of attending this brand new school outweighed potential risks. In order to minimize the economic barrier to a medical education, tuition was established at $500 a year for Kentucky residents and $950 for non-residents. (In comparison the 1995 tuition was $7,420 for Kentucky residents and $17,050 for non-residents.) This tuition was far below that charged by most medical schools at the time. It was justified in part by the hope that this would attract applicants from families of modest means and from less affluent areas of the state, and by the fact that, as a new school, the college had virtually no resources for offering scholarships or financial aid.

In selecting the first class, a heavy reliance was placed on the impressions gained from interviews with the applicants, most of whom had to endure being interviewed by several members of the committee as a group and by two members individually. For committee members, the students whom they selected and who enrolled were a very special class. They included only one woman and one black because, unfortunately, very few had applied. However, because the facilities had been designed to facilitate movement by handicapped persons (long before this was legally required) it was possible to admit a well qualified paraplegic student who had been turned down by several other schools.

There were several successful applicants who had been waiting for the school to open and had gained maturity in the process. One (William R. Markesbery who is now Director of the University of Kentucky's Center on Aging and a Professor of Neurology and Pathology) had a contract to play professional baseball when he applied. Another successful applicant had just been discharged after serving several years in the Navy. In his group interview he seemed reluctant to open his mouth. Only when Bill Knisely sized up the situation and used some raw "navy" language did the applicant relax and start talking (with a few raw words of his own). In keeping with its promise, the school admitted several students who had been undergraduate majors in the humanities or social sciences. Bill Markesbery has contrasted the warmth, respect and personal concern for him that he felt when he was interviewed at Kentucky with his experience at another school where he was faced with a "tribune" of three faculty members who actually sat on a raised platform when they interviewed him.

Because a few Kentucky applicants were attending college in the New York area, it was decided to save them the expense of travel by offering to interview them, along with some non-resident applicants, in a New York City hotel. Eight appointments were scheduled for one day and I was "elected" for this assignment. On arriving at the hotel in the evening I discovered large holes in both elbows of my sport jacket. Fortunately, there was a nearby Woolworths where I could purchase leather patches, needle and thread. I struggled, without a thimble, to sew patches on my coat while I interviewed the students. For those students who were nervous about their interview, I could not have planned a better "ice breaker" to help them relax.

DESIGNING THE CURRICULUM

Essentially the same people who served as an admissions committee put on "different hats" and along with Physiology Chairman Loren Carlson, set out to design the curriculum. This involved developing an overall plan for a four year curriculum and, within this framework, a detailed plan for the first year curriculum that would begin in September 1960.

Before discussing the curriculum that was developed for the first year, it is appropriate to consider the committee and the context. All of the members of this group were relatively young. They had been recommended by people who were generally familiar with Dr. Willard's philosophy, goals and aspirations for Kentucky. They all had already demonstrated excellence in both teaching and research, and the clinicians, in patient care. All were interested in innovation and experimentation. In agreeing to come to a new school and one that promised to be different, all were risk takers. All said that they had been captivated by Bill Willard personally and by his plans and his aspirations. Working in makeshift office space above the College of Agriculture's animal display pavilion, they had tackled the tasks of recruiting faculty members for their own departments, working with the architects to develop detailed designs for their own research and teaching laboratories, ordering technical equipment, joining the planning staff for meetings on general policy, selecting an initial class of students, and helping their families get settled in Lexington. In addition, within a short time after moving to Lexington, Bill Knisely, Ed Pellegrino, George Schwert and Loren Carlson had all submitted applications to the NIH for research grant support. All had received approval and funding and had successfully launched their research programs.

It was perhaps not by coincidence that Bill Knisely, George Schwert and Joseph Parker had each been recruited from Duke; all had been inspired and influenced by Eugene Stead, Duke's Chairman of Medicine and a man who shared many of Bill Willard's values and aspirations for medical education. All of the members of Kentucky's first curriculum committee were committed to change. The major goals of the committee can be summarized as follows: 1) to reduce the number of hours devoted to each of the traditional disciplines in the first year; 2) to increase the overall usefulness of unscheduled hours giving students more time for both learning and living; 3) to reduce the amount of time devoted to lecturing for memorization and regurgitation and increase the amount of time available for exploration and problem solving; 4) to increase opportunities for learning in the small group seminar type setting where students are encouraged to share their knowledge and teach each other; 5) to plan certain courses with parallel sequences so that students could study, for example, the anatomical, physiological and chemical aspects of the same phenomena at the same time; 6) to bring beginning medical students into contact with clinical medicine with experiences appropriate to their own educational development and with special emphasis on the application of basic science knowledge to clinical considerations; 7) to recognize the relevance to medicine of the content and methods of the social and behavioral sciences both through discrete courses and by including these considerations in a multidiscipline perspective; 8) to recognize the health needs, expectations and culture of Kentucky's people; and 9) to foster a multidiscipline perspective through a number of courses planned and taught jointly by faculty from several departments.

A number of architectural decisions that were essential for curriculum change had been made quite early in the planning process. These included the decision to provide a generous number of seminar rooms and the decision to design multipurpose student laboratories with adjacent seminar space that would both permit and require a significant departure from the traditional methods of laboratory teaching. In order to demonstrate and facilitate the non-intrusive inclusion of patients in the education of first year students, a lecture hall and several other spaces were equipped with one way glass.

In the initial first year curriculum that emerged, although the total number of schedule hours (1,163) represented a reduction of only about 100 hours from the mean of other schools, there were numerous innovations. The number of hours allotted to the traditional subjects — anatomy, biochemistry, and physiology — was substantially reduced. The schedule of classes assured each student at least two totally free afternoons during the week. About 40 percent of the scheduled time was devoted to conjoint multidisciplinary courses taught by groups of faculty from several departments. The social and behavioral sciences were represented in a course called Health and Society and in conjoint courses on human growth and development and on communication and interviewing (another innovation at that time). Over 100 hours in the curriculum were devoted to a conjoint course designed to help students begin to integrate the basic sciences with clinical problem solving and to have some contact with patients. Held every Saturday morning this became a favorite course with first-year students because it brought them in contact with patients, some of whom had fascinating health histories to share. A radical innovation was the decision to defer the systematic teaching of gross anatomy until the third year.

College curricula have often been compared with jigsaw puzzles. If this is an appropriate analogy, the curriculum that was developed for Kentucky's first medical school class's first year was a multi-dimensional jigsaw puzzle. Its implementation and success would require that faculty members be flexible in many ways. In lecturing they would have to accomplish more in fewer hours. They would have to learn to bring their laboratory instruction to the students. Many would have to learn for the first time how to guide constructively discussion among small groups of students; how to guide students in learning rather than just teaching them. Perhaps their greatest challenge would be to adapt to group teaching with colleagues from other departments and disciplines.

We developed the curriculum using what we called our "tabletop computer." We never dreamed then that a genuine tabletop computer would one day be a reality. Our "machine" was simply a large table on which we could arrange and rearrange 3" x 5" file cards representing various components of the curriculum.

Working with the college's first curriculum committee was an entirely gratifying experience because all of my colleagues shared common goals and were determined to reach them. Yet each had to go through the painful experience of giving up what for many were sacred departmental teaching hours in order to get the pieces of the puzzle to fit. I will never forget the afternoon that George Schwert agreed that somehow or other biochemistry could be taught with 20 fewer hours than he had been allotted. We suddenly realized that with this concession the pieces of our puzzle were finally all in place.

Once the general design of the curriculum was completed, members of the committee had to provide leadership for the faculty members they had recruited or would be recruiting, all of whom would have to implement their own particular teaching roles. During the years of planning, the philosophy of medical education and later the curriculum plan played a major role in the process of faculty recruitment. Many of the first faculty members recruited by Knisely, Schwert, Carlson, Pellegrino and others came to the University of Kentucky because they were attracted by the philosophy and curriculum. Conversely, others were not invited or did not accept because of philosophical differences or because they were disinclined to change their ways. Later, in anticipation of the arrival of subsequent classes of students and of hospital patients, there would be pressures to recruit faculty more rapidly and less selectively.

At the same time that student selection, curriculum design and faculty recruitment were going forward, many other activities were involved in the planning and development process. Hospital design was completed and construction underway, an administrative structure was developed for the College of Medicine and the Medical Center. Support staff were added. Specific agreements for relating the Medical Center and its colleges to the rest of the University were determined. Plans were developed and initiated for relating a functioning Medical Center to the communities and people of the State and a committee was formed to develop guidelines for programs of patient care. In December 1959, the basic science building was completed and made ready for occupancy by the growing body of faculty and staff who, by this time, were scattered and crowded in whatever space could be begged, borrowed or sequestered around the campus or the community. The large task of equipping laboratories and offices and preparing for the arrival of students could begin.

THE MEDICAL SCHOOL IS BORN

As 1959, and Happy Chandler's term as Governor drew to a close, Governor Chandler had indeed delivered on his promise to "build" a Medical Center at the University of Kentucky. Without compromising, the General Assembly had approved each of his requests for appropriations of State funds totaling 11 million dollars. An additional 6 million dollars in state funds was appropriated after Chandler was succeeded as Governor by Bert Combs who supported Chandler's recommendation. Matched with 11 million dollars in Federal grants, these were sufficient to build and partially equip the Medical Science Building, the connecting University Hospital and the Dental Science Wing. In recognition, the Board of Trustees of the University voted to honor Chandler by approving the name - Albert B. Chandler Medical Center.

Chandler was succeeded as Governor by Judge Bert T. Combs, leader of the rival faction of the Democratic Party. Chandler had defeated Combs in the gubernatorial primary election of 1955 and Combs in turn defeated the candidate Chandler was backing in the primaries of 1959. Neither man tried to hide the fact that they were bitter political enemies. Nor was it any secret that, given the political climate in the State at that time, there were some individuals who hoped that associating Chandler's name with the Medical Center would compromise the Center in its forthcoming negotiations with a new State administration for an initial operating budget and that the new administration would reign in some of the latitude that Dr. Willard had been accorded.

Fortunately for the Medical Center, Bert Combs was a man who shared Chandler's deep concern about the shortage and maldistribution of physicians and other health personnel in Kentucky and the limited access to health care for rural and economically deprived Kentuckians. Combs quickly demonstrated

127

that he would put the needs and well being of Kentuckians above political animosities. He made it clear that better education, adequate roads and improved health care were all high on his administration's agenda. The operating budgets that he recommended for the Medical Center during his four years in office made it possible for the College of Medicine to continue recruiting a well qualified faculty, quickly meet standards for full accreditation, and attract national attention for its innovative programs.

A few days after Governor Combs was inaugurated, I happened to be in Bill Willard's office when a call came through from the Governor. Bert Combs was calling with two messages. First he told Dr. Willard (what he already knew) that Governors receive many requests to intervene on behalf of applicants for medical school. The Governor then went on to say that he would be writing letters on behalf of such candidates. However, he recognized that the Medical School must select only fully qualified candidates and Dr. Willard should feel under no obligation to honor his "recommendations."

In his subsequent relationships with the Chandler Medical Center, Governor Bert Combs was a gracious and supportive advocate for quality medical education. At the ceremonies dedicating the Medical Center on September 23, 1960, Combs praised Chandler as the man "whose vision and perseverance constituted the driving force for transforming a wonderful dream into a wonderful fact." Referring to people who said that Kentucky could not afford the Center, Combs added "I say we can afford it. Actually, Kentucky cannot afford not to have it." Lexington's newspapers, that had long supported the need for a medical school at the University of Kentucky, both celebrated the school's opening. Herndon J. Evans, editor of the Lexington *Herald* wrote that "Kentucky is realizing the fulfillment of a dream that will mean much to the future of our state" (September 9, 1960). Fred B. Wachs, editor of the Lexington *Leader* noted "It has been a long and difficult road, but the planning has been wise and sound, and there is every reason to believe that here in Lexington we will have one of the foremost and certainly one of the most modern medical centers in the entire country. ...We have something here of which all Kentuckians should be proud" (September 15, 1960).

In a complete turn around of an earlier editorial position, Russell Briney, the editor of the Louisville *Courier-Journal* wrote that the Medical Center's dedication marked "a great day for the people of Kentucky ... marking a major milestone in the effort of the state to provide the finest medical education for its young people (and) the most modern medical care for all of its citizens." He added that "with the start of classes in its new medical school ... the University of Kentucky can be said to have come of age." Referring to the University of Louisville's medical school the editorial praised "a spirit of friendly rivalry between the schools ... as well as a feeling of earnest cooperation. This bodes well" (The Louisville *Courier-Journal*, September 26, 1960).

In addition to the dedication ceremonies, the opening of the College of Medicine was celebrated by the making of 30 minute, color format, film entitled "A School for Doctors." Sponsored by the Southern Medical Association for viewing at their annual convention, the film was narrated by the well known commentator John Cameron Swayze. The script began with Swayze's melodious voice — "In Lexington, Kentucky, there is a field of corn. Once it stretched as far as the eye could see ... but in the year nineteen sixty, the farm land became the scene of a near miracle." With Bob Johnson serving as laison to the film-makers, a script was developed that caught the spirit of the school's purpose and the combination of forces and people that were required to make it a reality. Following its "opening night" at the Association's convention in Saint Louis, the film was shown for many years, in the words of Bob Johnson, "to every group or organization in Kentucky that will give us a chance."

The years 1956-1960, devoted to planning and preparation for activation, were years of "becoming" for the College of Medicine. With the official dedication and the arrival of the first students in September 1960, the College experienced its "beginning."

Chapter Six will follow the College's beginning through the first half of the 1960s as it moved rapidly toward full activation.

The "original" College of Medicine. Freeman House, a small residence that stood near the northeast corner of the University's agricultural farm was the first College of Medicine office building.
By the time that the medical science building was ready
for occupancy in December 1959, more than 20 people were crowded into its rooms and corridors.

Building blocks. After the major pieces of the Medical Center and their shape had been determined, these walnut blocks were used to help the people of Kentucky envision their future University Medical Center.

Picture postcard. This artist's drawing of the future Medical Center provided a colorful preview of things to come. Note that the hospital has been shown with 12 floors instead of 8.

Digging down. Excavation is under way for the medical science building.

Going up. Pouring concrete for the fourth floor.

"Here it is!" Dr. Willard showing the walnut building
block model of the future medical center to
Dr. Richard G. Elliott, President
of the Fayette County Medical Society.

Plotting and planning. From the left - Alan Ross, Bob McCafferty, Bill Knisely, Bob Straus, Bill Willard, Joseph Parker, Ed Pellegrino and George Schwert in the finished but still unfurnished Dean's office.

*Treasure trove. Russell White, Dick Noback, Brick Chambers
and medical librarian, Alfred Brandon unpacking the collection
of journals acquired from the Wistar Institute.*

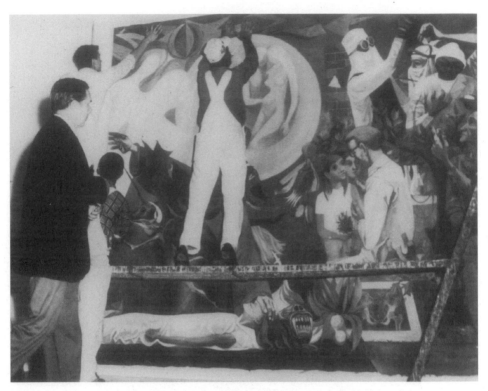

Finishing touch. Installing the Refregier mural in the medical school's lobby.

A solemn moment. Governors Albert B. Chandler and Bert Combs, Emeritus President Herman Donovan, and others look on as President Frank Dickey convenes a convocation marking the opening of the College of Medicine.

A happy day. Dr. Willard and Governor Chandler share their fulfillment as College of Medicine is dedicated.

Friendly rivals. Although they were political "enemies" Governors Chandler and Combs were both strong supporters of the University of Kentucky Medical Center and its College of Medicine. Here they share the pleasures of dedication day with President Frank Dickey.

A campus location. When the Medical Center was viewed from the south, its location adjacent to the rest of the University's campus is apparent. Most buildings on the main campus can been seen in the upper left.

A cornfield. When viewed from the west, the former cornfield's pastoral location on a corner of the University's agricultural farm is apparent.

Chapter Six

FOR THE STUDENT,
THE PATIENT
AND THE PEOPLE

When, in September 1960, students arrived to enroll in the College of Medicine's first class, they each received a key to the medical science building. This was intended in part as a symbolic gesture; a way of emphasizing that the medical school had been created for its students. (Keys would be needed for night access until the activation of the University Hospital in 1962, after which the building would be open around the clock.) The keys were also intended to convey the message that students were free to adapt their use of the college facilities to their own personal work schedules and lifestyles.

In the original design, student space figured significantly in the configuration of the medical center. Past experiences of the planning staff indicated that most medical students feel that they never have enough time. One obvious approach to alleviating some of the time pressure that medical students experience was to redesign the curriculum. Another was to provide facilities that would help students make the most efficient use of the time that they had. This involved making a significant investment in space and equipment. Each student was provided with a personal study area consisting of desk, bookcase, file drawer and locker for clothes and equipment. Each student, for the first two years, also had a personal laboratory area. These student labs were clustered in groups of sixteen with adjacent seminar space for both formal teaching and informal discussion. They were also designed so that the laboratory portions of courses in biochemistry, physiology and pharmacology could all be taught on the students' rather than the faculty members' turf. For students in the third and fourth years, each hospital floor had a laboratory specially designated for students and house officers. Other provisions for students included a spacious, comfortably furnished lounge, shower stalls in one restroom, and (until the hospital food service was activated) a room of vending machines stocked with more variety than traditional snacks and soft drinks.

The faculty members who launched the College of Medicine reflected Dr. Willard's intentions to "put the students first." Many worked with open doors and were available to discuss personal as well as academic problems when students sought them out. Faculty offices and department seminar rooms were often available at night for students who needed to study by themselves or in groups.

Although when the College opened there were few resources of financial aid, the very low tuition for a medical school ($500 for Kentucky residents) was designed to minimize the students' financial burden. In addition the $500 microscopes that each student would need were purchased by the school and rented to the students for a nominal fee.

For student physical activity and recreation, a half basketball court was provided in a (soon to be inadequate) parking lot. The only significant missing ingredient was a student dormitory. Plans to seek funds for such a facility were dropped when it became apparent that most medical students preferred to live in private off-campus facilities and when general university housing became available to those who wanted it. About 12 medical students were able to live without charge in a house provided by a group of Lexington physicians.

These various facilities for students also reflected recognition of and respect for individual variability in students' personal study habits and even in their individual biological clocks. The goal was to enable each student to adapt the resources of the college to his or her most effective way of studying and living. The individuality that students demonstrated, given this opportunity, exceeded the most extreme expectations. A few students found that they worked most effectively by leaving the College in the late afternoon, sleeping in the evening and early morning hours, and coming back to the College at 3 or 4:00 a.m. for several hours of quiet, uninterrupted study at a time when they found their ability to concentrate and think sharply was maximized. Some favored working until late at night and sleeping in the early hours of the morning. Others, when they felt pressured, liked to work all night long, sometimes interspersing study with "catnaps." Before the year was very far along, at least one student decided that he did not need a place to "live" and gave up his rented room. It was discovered that he was quite contentedly meeting all of his personal and student needs without going out the doors of the Medical Center. In his case the facilities were providing an unanticipated form of "academic freedom."

Bill Markesbery (Director of the Center on Aging) who was a member of the class of 1964 has described his initial impressions of the College. According to Bill, the faculty "were well organized and prepared." There was "warmth" in the classroom and the students "were made to feel special." There was "clarity to the teaching" with "much emphasis on underlying concepts." Bill also remembers being amazed by the "outstanding depth" in the Medical Library and by its "user friendly, welcoming and helpful staff." (Personal comunication.)

THE COLLEGE OF MEDICINE
AND THE UNIVERSITY

Basic to the founding philosophy was the conviction that a college of medicine and an academic medical center would derive great strength from close integration with a university. It was this conviction that supported locating the Medical Center as close to the rest of the University campus as possible rather than having a separate medical campus some distance away.

Although by the very nature of medical education the College of Medicine had many requirements that were "different" and seemed to set the medical complex apart, there were also many aspects of "integration." Basic science courses in the College of Medicine were open to graduate students from other departments of the University. The medical college curriculum included courses of varying length and was designed to permit logical sequencing and interfacing. For these reasons it did not follow a regular semester format. However, it was designed so that medical students could take elective courses in other parts of the University. Beginning with the Department of Sociology, a pattern was established that encouraged and facilitated joint faculty appointments for medical faculty in other university departments and the reverse. Long before the College of Medicine was activated, some of its faculty members were serving on university wide committees.

Loren Carlson and his Department of Physiology invited members of an entire department from the College of Arts and Sciences to join the College of Medicine faculty. Loren had come to Kentucky from the University of Washington where he had served as Assistant Dean for Education in the medical school and also as Director of General Education for the University. He brought a strong commitment to cultivating close ties between the College of Medicine and other units of the University.

The Medical Library, from the day that Alfred Brandon arrived from California with a station wagon load of books and journals, was envisioned as a resource for the entire University and as a unit in the University library system. Responsibility for the University's Student Health Center was assumed by the Medical Center in 1957 and as soon as facilities were available it was located within the Medical Center complex.

The Graduate School was an immediate focus of integration. The Dean of the Graduate School and other university faculty members were invited to participate in medical faculty recruitment and, as they were recruited, most basic science and some clinical faculty members of the College of Medicine were invited to become members of the Graduate Faculty.

Although, as noted earlier, there were areas of stress and contention with respect to some business matters and there was conflict on the academic side with respect to microbiology, thanks to the example and expectations set by President Dickey and Dr. Willard and the good will and positive approach of a large number of faculty members, precedents were established whereby the University and the College of Medicine could, from the very beginning, derive strength from each other.

Looking back on the impact of the Medical Center on the University, historian Carl Cone would write in 1992: "The medical center contributed a sense of maturity and professionalism that had not existed previously. Graduate programs were stimulated and the university acquired a new character. No longer, as before 1960, could it be considered an undergraduate institution in which research, graduate and professional studies were of secondary importance." (Carl B. Cone. "University of Kentucky" in John E. Kleber, ed., *The Kentucky Encyclopedia*, Lexington: University Press of Kentucky, 1992.)

A HOSPITAL FOR STUDENTS AND PATIENTS

During the planning process, visits had been made to more than half of the existing medical schools in the country, looking for advice regarding innovations that were working and deficiencies that should be avoided. It quickly became apparent that there were glaring deficiencies in the design of hospitals, including university owned and operated hospitals, with respect to provisions for teaching, considerations for patient care that went beyond the technical aspects, and provisions for the comfort of patients' families. In response to their question "what would you do differently," planning staff members were repeatedly advised of the need for spaces for communicating with students outside of patients' rooms, and for communicating in privacy with patients or their family members. They found that few hospitals provided designated spaces where students could examine charts, study, or carry out their clinical laboratory assignments. Equally rare were provisions for physicians to confer with each other or with patients or their family members away from the bedside or public corridor. Provisions for family members were often thoughtlessly inadequate, overcrowded, uncomfortably furnished and lacking easy access to such necessities as rest rooms, water fountains, and telephones. Because of their design, many teaching hospitals exposed students to examples of inconsideration for the feelings, anxieties, and emotional needs of patients and their family members. I had become personally sensitive to the absence of provisions for hospital visitors at the birth of our first child in 1946. During an all night vigil, a fellow father-to-be and I wandered the deserted corridors of Yale's New Haven Hospital looking unsuccessfully for an unlocked men's room, a working water fountain, something to eat, and a telephone.

The original design for Kentucky's University Hospital included many provisions that reflected a reaction to these widespread deficiencies. Each floor of the hospital was provided with a student laboratory and a seminar/conference room where students also might study. Nursing stations were designed with space for medical students to work on charts. Each floor was provided with at least two small rooms where physicians could confer privately with patients (if ambulant), with family members, with students or with each other. Waiting areas included rest rooms, water fountains, and telephones and directions to other resources were provided by color coded lines in the corridor floors.

Because most of the architectural decisions had to be made before key clinical personnel were recruited and before detailed planning for programs of patient care and clinical education could take place, they were primarily influenced by the statement of Philosophy of Medical Education and by the visits that were made to other academic medical centers. These architectural decisions would provide both opportunities and limitations for those who would eventually plan in detail the programs for patient care and for the experiences of patients and students.

From their visits to other Kentucky hospitals, and from the study of responses to illness that were part of the planning process, it had become apparent that among many Kentucky families, when one member was hospitalized, the whole family would accompany the sick member to the hospital. This custom was particularly prevalent in the small towns and rural areas but was also common when family members from these areas were hospitalized in Lexington or Louisville. Because, in the 1960s, a majority of these patients came from fairly large families where they were accustomed to sharing bedrooms and even beds, many were extremely anxious about the thought of being placed in a room or a bed by themselves. From the perspective of such patients and their families the worst time for them to be left alone was when they were sick. In recognition of this custom, the University Hospital was planned with what were assumed to be ample waiting areas and they were comfortably furnished. It was also projected that the hospital's visiting hours would be very liberal and that the responsibilities of the hospital's social service department would include arranging temporary housing for patients' families in nearby rooming houses or motels. But the planners failed to recognize the intensity with which many patients would fear being left alone and the tenacity with which their kinfolk would stand by them. Within a short time after the hospital opened, the medical and nursing staffs and others responsible for patient care policy would be faced with several unanticipated questions such as: What to do about spouses or other relatives who slipped into the patients' rooms in order to share their beds for the night? How to respond when large families took over entire waiting areas? How to deal with visitors who slept on the floors of waiting rooms, corridors, the hospital lobby or even restrooms and staircase landings? These questions illustrate an area in which initial intentions and policies would have to be modified to meet needs or situations that were not anticipated in the planning process.

We came to regret two decisions that were made in designing the hospital, both for reasons of economy. We provided only one single room on each 20 bed nursing unit. This was not enough to meet the requirements of good medical care and was insufficient to provide for the preferences of fully paying patients. We also rejected, because it would reduce the number of beds we could have, the consulting architects' proposal for a circular wing that would afford ready visibility and access between a central nursing station and patients' rooms. Such a design, although radical at that time, is now considered "state of the art." On the bright side, after hearing many complaints about windowless hospital cafeterias located in low ceilinged basements, we were able to locate our cafeteria on the first floor with spacious windows on two sides.

Another feature of hospital planning that was distinctive for its time was a provision for progressive levels of care - intensive, general and ambulatory. The hospital was one of the first in the country to have areas especially designed to provide intensive care for patients whose condition was critical, a feature that is now standard in hospital design. At the other end of the spectrum, it was initially intended to devote part of the north wing of the hospital to patients whose condition did not require standard hospital care. These might be patients undergoing diagnosis or those no longer requiring standard nursing or observation but not yet ready for discharge.

Early in the planning process, consideration was given to trying to make the patient care services of the medical center more readily available. For example, it was initially proposed that all functions of the hospital be fully operational seven days a week, rather than follow the prevailing hospital practice of partially shutting down on weekends. In this way, it was argued, the availability of hospital services would be more in line with the schedule of needs for them and the investment in the physical plant and expensive equipment would be more fully utilized. It was also proposed that outpatient services be available at least six days a week and that their hours be extended into the evenings. These intentions were never implemented because it became apparent that we could not recruit enough professional or supporting personnel who would be willing to work the required hours.

In keeping with a commitment to the practice and teaching of comprehensive medicine, the hospital was initially planned to provide undifferentiated (medical and surgical) services in most of its patient care areas. Under this arrangement, following an initial evaluation by a member of the Department of Medicine, patients would be cared for by a surgeon, an internest or both as their needs dictated and a psychiatrist would be available for consultations, if necesssary. As will be discussed later in this chapter this too proved to be unacceptable to some of those who were responsible for its implementation.

RECOGNIZING AESTHETIC EXPRESSION
AND SPIRITUAL NEEDS

In the overall design of the Medical Center major emphasis was placed on function and economy of form, rather than on aesthetics. Thus, most interior walls were merely painted cinder blocks, most research and teaching rooms were without finished ceilings, floors were tiled rather than carpeted, and the exterior was faced with red brick rather than the marble that the architect had suggested. A major goal in design was to maximize the net space in relation to gross space. Yet, it was deemed important to provide for aesthetic expression that would represent medicine as a form of art as well as science and the history of medical thought and practice as inseparable from other aspects of human culture and history. To this end, three works of art were commissioned.

For the front of the hospital, facing Rose Street, there is a granite inlay mural designed by Richard Haines of the Otis Art Institute in Los Angeles. Based on the general theme "Science of Man," the mural is designed to represent biological, historical, sociological, psychological and philosophical components of medicine. There are four panels each 16 feet high and 20 feet wide. The first panel represents the family and its basic needs for food, shelter, fire, and security. The second panel portrays sociological and historical processes; teaching, learning, communication, group activity, superstitions, traditions, and heredity. The third panel represents the continuing search for new knowledge about the human body and mind. And the fourth panel portrays the dissemination of new knowledge and the exchange and evaluation of ideas, both scientific and philosophical. Originally placed on the front wall of the hospital itself, the mural was moved at a time of hospital expansion to a specially constructed wall where it continues to represent the Medical Center's face to the community.

Best known of the art work is a sculpture intended to represent the duality of humankind. Intertwined are a rising and a descending form, each with a dual interpretation. Under one interpretation, the rising form represents the heights that humans have reached while the descending form represents human mediocrity, failures and disappointments. The other interpretation (preferred by this author) has the rising form representing aspirations, opportunities and achievements of the future while the descending form represents the wisdom that has been derived from the past. Designed by Amarigo Brioschi, of St. Paul, Minnesota, the sculpture took nine months to complete, is 28 feet high and weighs 10 tons. It consists of a stainless steel frame covered with concrete and an outer shell of black granite and quartz. Originally the statue was placed in the middle of a circular fountain and pool in front of the Medical Center. Due to new construction, it has been moved twice and is now the centerpiece of the North courtyard. Striking in its form, the statue was used for many years as a model for the Medical Center logo. This was despite the fact that, ever since its unveiling, the statue has been popularly known as the "copulating boomerangs."

In the main lobby of the medical science building there is a large oil on canvas mural by Anton Refregier. This is an intricate and colorful work that is intended to depict the human quest for knowledge about our bodies, minds and health.

Because of the austerity under which the University was operating in the late 1950s, and the economy that was maintained in the Medical Center design, the decision to commission these distinctive works of art that was carefully reviewed and approved by the University Board of Trustees, symbolized a new level of aspiration for the entire University.

Somewhat related to the investment in works of art was a decision to provide in the hospital a suitable place where students, staff, patients and visitors might meet their spiritual needs, find solace or simply retreat. An advisory committee that included several representatives from the religious community was asked to make recommendations regarding the functions and scope of such a facility. Suggestions that ranged from the grandiose (150 seats) to the very modest (15 seats) led to the design of a small aesthetically pleasing chapel suitable to the needs of all major faiths and so located that it could be expanded to incorporate the space of an adjacent hallway should a particular function so indicate.

THE INITIAL CURRICULUM

When Dr. Willard greeted the first class of medical students on their day of arrival in 1960 he told them that they would be beginning a process of lifelong learning. He referred to rapidly accelerating rates of change in medical knowledge, technology, methods of delivering medical care, and the nature of society. All of these changes and more, he told them, would affect every aspect of their professional lives. He told them, too, that they would be experiencing a curriculum designed to help them cope with change and begin their process of lifelong learning; a curriculum that would place an emphasis on concepts and problem solving so that they could use the knowledge they had to identify questions and know where to seek answers. He said they would be learning about the behavioral as well as the biological sciences, about communication and ethics, about how the health problems of people effect their total lives, and how community resources are mobilized to meet health needs. All of this, he said, would be basic to their preparing for the practice of comprehensive health care.

As noted in Chapter Five, the plan that was developed for the first year curriculum included a reduction in the time traditionally allotted for discipline oriented courses that were taught by specific departments and the allocation of about 40 percent of the time to conjoint courses that cut across several disciplines and were taught by committees of faculty drawn from several departments. The plan called for laboratory teaching (except anatomy) to take place around the students' personal laboratory units. The curriculum included the introduction of clinical applications, exposure to patients, instruction about communication and the incorporation of the social and behavioral sciences. In developing this curriculum, much thought was given to identifying the contents of traditional curricula that students really did not have to know as well as what was essential.

In order to make it possible for students who so desired to take other University courses, two afternoons a week were left unscheduled. Unfortunately, this option had few users because most students felt that they could not take the time away from their medical studies. One elective offering that did attract many students and faculty as well was an evening seminar on medical ethics organized by Ed Pellegrino. The philosophy statement had stressed the goal of minimizing the examination process in order to reduce the pressures and anxieties often associated with exams. It soon became apparent that many students tended to be anxious without regular exams. They wanted to know where they stood. Many of the faculty also were uneasy. Despite the fact that the curriculum gave them opportunities to interact with students on a one to one basis, they felt that they needed exams to complete their evaluations of student progress.

During the College's first year of activation most of the faculty took the time to sit in on some of the teaching by other departments so that they could know first hand what the students were learning. Although practice was seldom followed after the first year when the pressure of additional classes of students, grant funded research and (for clinicians) patient care responsibilities made such faculty learning a "luxury," it was particularly helpful in establishing credibility for the behavioral success. The Department of Behavioral Science often had 10 or 12 other faculty sitting in on its teaching sessions and its relevance for the students was reinforced when Bill Knisely, Ed Pellegrino and others, as they often did, referred to behavioral concepts in their own teaching. I attended other courses as often as possible, trying to learn what the students were learning and how they were being taught. I especially admired Bill Knisely's insistence on respect for the human cadaver as his way of teaching medical ethics and his recruiting a faculty of dedicated and skillful teachers and establishing a truly student oriented department. The conjoint courses, since they were the responsibility of interdepartmental committees and cut across traditional discipline lines, all required considerable time for planning. In the beginning most of the faculty seemed to enjoy these sessions but they too became burdensome as the time pressures from other activities increased.

The initial curriculum that was developed for second year students, like that of the first year included about 40 percent of the scheduled time in conjoint courses. However, most of these were conjoint for administrative rather than multidisciplinary reasons. Two of the conjoint courses, "Fundamentals of Microbiology and Infectious Disease" and "Parasitic Diseases of Man" were developed because the policy of "departmental unity" had been invoked to block the establishment of a microbiology department in the College of Medicine. A conjoint course called Physiology and Biochemistry of Drug Action was developed in place of traditional Pharmacology primarily because a chairman for Pharmacology had not yet been recruited.

A course in Community Medicine, entirely new to medical education, replaced the traditional teaching of public health and preventive medicine. Courses in Medical Diagnosis, Radiobiology, Psychopathology of Behavior, and Pathology rounded out the second year.

In keeping with the philosophy of teaching comprehensive medicine to undergraduate medical students, the original curriculum plan for the third year provided for a 12 week general adult clerkship and a 12 week general children's clerkship with the intention that medical, surgical and psychiatric considerations of patients' conditions would be considered conjointly and that students would be assigned to teams of attending physicians. Plans for the third year also provided for separate 6-week clerkships in psychiatry and obstetrics, and provisions for weekly case management conferences that would include representatives from nursing, social service, pharmacy, rehabilitation personnel, and behavioral science in addition to medical specialists. Totally innovative for medical education, the third year began with a course in dissection and regional anatomy, subjects that were traditionally being taught in the first year by other medical schools.

The fourth year provided for 13 weeks each devoted to

introductions for the medical and surgical specialties including experiences in both outpatient and inpatient settings. Additionally there was a 4-week community medicine experience away from the College of Medicine and a flexible 16-week period for scheduling a vacation and elective courses.

The initial planning for each year of the curriculum involved input from members of the planning staff, departmental chairmen as they were recruited, and, as time went on, faculty members who the chairmen had in turn recruited. At this stage all of those involved where fully aware of and most had been attracted by the Philosophy of Medical Education statement. Most aspects of the initial curriculum for each year reflected the principles and goals set forth in the philosophy statement. They represented many departures from the traditional curricula that were being followed by almost every medical school in the country at that time.

These innovations included:

A reduction in the number of lectures in the basic sciences.

The relocation of the major gross anatomy course to the third year.

The introduction of a course on communication and interviewing.

Courses in the behavioral sciences taught by the first Department of Behavioral Science in a medical school. (Ten years later, the National Board of Medical Examiners would begin to include a section on the behavioral sciences in its Part I examinations.)

The development of several conjoint courses taught by committees of faculty from several departments and disciplines.

Courses in community medicine taught by the first Department of Community Medicine in a medical school, an innovation that would soon be emulated by many other schools.

Laboratory teaching located in the students' own laboratory units with faculty from several departments coming to the students.

Major clinical teaching provided on undifferentiated clinical services by teams representing medicine, surgery and psychiatry.

Conferences on comprehensive medicine that included representatives from nursing, social work, pharmacy, behavioral science, dietetics as well as physicians.

As will be seen later in this chapter, comparable innovations were included in the planning for patient care.

Some of the medical students who comprised the College's first class were not completely happy about all of the departures from tradition. Most had friends who were going to other medical schools so they were well aware of the fact that Kentucky was going to be different. Some had discussed their medical education with their own physicians or physician friends of their families many of whom expressed surprise and concern when they learned for example that there would be no dissection course in gross anatomy in the first year. Gross was "always" taught in the first year. Their insecurities were exacerbated when they went home for vacations, compared notes with their peers, and learned how very different the Kentucky curriculum was. According to several members of this first class, even though, to the surprise of some of them, they passed both parts of the National Board exams, they were very apprehensive about how they would perform in their internships and residencies. Yet, most were pleasantly surprised to find that they did very well. Evaluations of these graduates were solicited by the College and virtually all ranged from positive to very positive.

Drs. William T. Maxson and William R. Markesbery of the class of 1964, have each told me of their anxieties when they went from Kentucky to residencies at Johns Hopkins (Maxson) and Columbia (Markesbery). Despite his apprehension about how he would fare, Bill Maxson soon found that he was better prepared for the program at Hopkins than his peers who came from more prestigious and well established schools. He credits this to that fact that the Kentucky curriculum reflected a consideration of what students did not have to know as well as what they needed to know. Unlike some other schools, Kentucky had encouraged students to use the knowledge they had to reason through solutions to problems. Of course, Bill Maxson was describing "problem based learning," a technique that was used by some faculty at Kentucky long before the term was coined and the method of instruction became popularized in medical education. Bill Markesbery credits Kentucky with emphasizing the understanding of facts in relation to function rather than just memorization. He remembers a significant amount of small group and individual teaching and a faculty that "set high standards, exemplified a work ethic and tried to decrease the students' anxiety and build their confidence." (Personal communications with Drs. Maxson and Markesbery.)

PATIENT CARE - A MODEL FOR TEACHING

When the Medical Center was conceived, the most persuasive argument for having a university hospital was to enable medical students to learn the practice of medicine in a setting that would be oriented to the needs of education and in which academic control could insure that students would be exposed to an appropriate distribution of problems and patients and to examples of exemplary patient care. From the beginning too, as documented by Chapter Four, the College was committed to the practice and teaching of comprehensive medicine.

Toward the end of 1959, the major tasks of securing funding for and designing the medical center buildings had been accomplished and construction was underway. The recruitment of key faculty was in full progress. Criteria for the selection of students had been developed and curriculum planning had been initiated. With the anticipated completion of a university hospital about two years away, serious attention was turned to preparing for the realities and responsibilities of hospital operation and caring for patients.

A Committee on Hospital Organization for Clinical Teaching and Patient Care was formed, chaired by Edmund D. Pellegrino, Professor and Chairman of the Department of Medicine. Ed Pellegrino brought to this role a unique combination of professional qualifications and personal qualities. He was a humanist, ethicist, and classical scholar; a skilled diagnostician and clinician, a compassionate physician, a gifted teacher and an admirable role model. In the planning process, Ed's great strength lay in his ability to see all sides of an issue, to respect those views that differed from his own and to seek a position that all could agree on. Ed's gift for achieving a satisfactory solution out of conflicting views made him a particularly effective chairman for the patient care committee faced as it was with evolving proposals for resolving a large number of issues on which there were differing viewpoints. However, in an effort to be fair and respectful of the positions of others and in order to achieve a resolution, Ed sometimes was faced with having to compromise his own positions.

The Committee began as a small group. In addition to Pellegrino and Willard, it included Dick Wittrup the hospital administrator, Dick Noback and Joe Parker from the clinical faculty, Bob Straus from behavioral science and curriculum planning, and representatives from hospital administration, hospital nursing and nursing education. As they were recruited, the chairmen of other clinical departments, the director for social service and a representative of dental education joined the group. Eventually, there were several sub-committees asked to consider such topics as hospital admissions, ambulatory care, the emergency room, the out-patient clinics, patient recreation, rehabilitation and patient care research.

As a frame of reference for patient care planning a staff memorandum entitled "Comprehensive Medicine: Its Applications to Patient Care and Clinical Teaching" had been prepared, with Ed Pellegrino as the primary author. In this memorandum, the difficulty of developing too detailed a plan without the participation of as yet to be recruited clinical chairmen and other key persons was acknowledged. The goal was to suggest specific points that would be considered "essential and irreducible," without giving the impression of a "fait accompli," yet while achieving "a proper balance between a too generalized approach and an overdetailed conceptualization so early in the course of events." It was acknowledged that with actual operational experience, modifications would be necessary.

Essential principles set forth in this planning document included:

1) A reorganization of clinical services along undifferentiated lines will result in improvement in all phases of patient care.

2) Education, research and service in the health field should be better served by a comprehensive approach to the patient's problems.

3) A "progressive care" plan must be incorporated into our clinical teaching and patient care projections.

4) All patients will be "teaching patients" and will have an attending physician.

5) The primary goal of full time faculty members in rendering service to patients and carrying out their practice is to maintain and increase their clinical skills so that they may be effective teachers.

6) Organizational arrangements should reduce to a minimum the barriers to interdisciplinary cooperation and provide the best possible opportunity for cooperative efforts.

7) Educational experiences should reduce to a minimumthe artificial separation that often exists between basic and clinical sciences and clinical disciplines themselves.

8) There is a firm intent to consider the patient totally as an individual, as a member of the family, and as a member of society and to consider health as of equal concern to medicine as its concern with disease.

9) A stated objective is the preparation of the "undifferentiated physician;" to provide a "liberal" education in medicine that would prepare the student with further training to enter any of the specialties or fields of medicine.

10) Emphasis will be on the inculcation of a way of thinking and an approach to clinical situations that emphasizes respect for the scientific method along with an understanding of the broader aspects of the patient's life.

11) Comprehensive medicine approaches the problems of health and disease from the broadest point of view; it is concerned with the best organization of available health resources around the needs of the individual, the family, and the community so as to provide care that is total, continuous and integrated.

12) Comprehensive medicine includes precise diagnosis, the institution of rational treatment, rehabilitation, prevention of similar future episodes, maintenance of general health, continuity of care and attention to the patient as a member of a family and of a society with recognition of problems associated with these roles.

13) Essential to the expression of comprehensive medicine is the team approach whereby all those involved with a patient's problems communicate and cooperate with each other for the patient's benefit. Yet, a team can be dehumanizing unless there is one individual clearly recognized by the patient as having primary responsibility for coordination and communication with the patient.

Hopefully, by bringing medical, surgical and psychiatric faculty members together physically, they would begin to work and teach conjointly along with the cooperating roles of nurses, social workers, psychologists, pharmacists, dieticians, physical and occupational therapists, and others, demonstrating for students team work and their roles therein.

In many respects, the process of planning for patient care involved the most complex and difficult aspects of the entire planning process. It brought into sharp focus the need to achieve an accommodation of ideals and pragmatic issues; it involved potential conflict among the traditions, the organizational patterns, and the cultures, as well as the practical requirements, of different medical specialties and different professions and the services they represented. It involved accommodations with respect to the use of space within the hospital and the conflicts associated with accommodating educational needs, to patient care needs and the varied responsibilities and working schedules of many categories of medical and supporting personnel.

By the time that the first patients were admitted to the University Hospital well over 100 individuals had contributed to the patient care committee's deliberations and recommendations and those of its sub committees. As time went by, the Committee successfully resolved literally hundreds of issues and questions. Some indication of the vastness of its task will be found in the following partial list of hospital functions for which planning was required:

Medical records	Radiology
Laboratory services	Patient Transport
Social service	House
Pharmacy and therapeutics	Blood Bank
Chaplaincy program	Operating Room
Food Service	Recovery Room
Tissue review	Research
Hospital infection	Clinical Pathology
Admission policies	Clinical Board
Pricing policies	Emergency Room

Patient recreation and diversion	Autopsies
Public information	Out-patient
Relating to Law Enforcement	department
Student Health Service	Security

By April of 1962 when the hospital admitted its first patients responsibilities had been delineated, policies adopted and personnel designated for each of the above listed functions and more. Nine clinical departments had been established in the College of Medicine with their chairmen designated as chiefs of service or directors for their corresponding hospital functions. Chairmen were installed for the departments of Medicine (Ed Pellegrino), Surgery (Ben Eiseman), Pediatrics (Jack Githens), Psychiatry (Joe Parker), Pathology (Wellington Stewart), Radiology and Radiation Medicine (Harold Rosenbaum) and Community Medicine (Kurt Deuschle). Peter Bosomworth, the chairman of Anesthesiology, arrived in Lexington just two days before the hospital opened. Activation of Obstetrics and Gynecology followed after the recruiting of its chairman Jack Greene.

Each of the original chairmen of the clinical departments placed his mark on the College of Medicine. Joe Parker brought an interest in integrating psychiatry with general medical care. Harold Rosenbaum developed a department that was and has remained in the forefront of rapidly changing technology and has been both student oriented and responsive to patients' needs. For thirty years, until his retirement, Harold personally taught the course in radiobiology by meeting with his students in groups of eight. Pete Stewart led the College into the early use of computer technology. Jack Githens effectively related the department of pediatrics to statewide needs. He established some of the college's earliest outreach clinics, and he also placed special emphasis on meeting the emotional as well as physical needs of pediatric patients and their parents. Jack Greene by his personal example inspired his department to be oriented to the needs of both students and patients. Peter Bosomworth developed a strong and well balanced department that included several future chairmen.

Ed Pellegrino's department of medicine included some faculty who followed his commitment to excellence in clinical care and teaching and others who were selected primarily for their research interests. Ed broke with tradition by appointing two general practitioners to tenure line faculty positions in his department. (One of these men, Joseph Hamburg, later became the founding dean of the College of Allied Health Sciences; the other, Nicholas Pisacano, became Director of the American Board of Family Practice which established its national headquarters in Lexington.) Ben Eiseman became such a significant force both in building the department of surgery and influencing the direction of the College's development that a brief profile is appropriate here.

Ben Eiseman was appointed Chairman of the Department of Surgery in June of 1961. Nothing would be quite the same from that day forth. Ben came to Lexington with remarkably impressive credentials. He was a graduate of Yale and the Harvard Medical School. He had been an intern at the Massachusetts General Hospital and a surgical resident at the Barnes Hospital of Washington University, two of the nation's most prestigious teaching hospitals. He then served on the faculty of Washington University's School of Medicine including a stint as assistant dean before going to the University of Colorado where he rose to the rank of professor and served a year as acting dean. He had been selected for membership by numerous prestigious medical and surgical societies and was about to become President of the Society of University Surgeons. In short, Ben Eiseman was a "top dog" when he arrived at Kentucky. Then, in a very short time, he assembled a faculty of amazingly impressive strength. Eight of the men he recruited to join him in Lexington were destined to become Chairmen of their own departments of surgery. As surgeons they demonstrated technical excellence and were at the forefront of advancements in their specialty. As an example they developed one of the nation's early programs for kidney transplant and the long-term survival rate of their patients was outstanding.

Ben had originally been suggested in 1958 by several of the local Lexington surgeons, including some of the school's strongest supporters. He had spent two days with the planning staff in 1958 serving as a consultant on the design of surgical facilities in the hospital. When he returned as a candidate for chairman of the department of surgery, he presented impressive credentials, had strong support from the surgical community, and demonstrated an obvious interest in providing and teaching technically exemplary surgical care. Although a majority of his internal advisors favored another candidate who appeared more interested in and committed to the philosophical goals of the College, Dr. Willard selected Eiseman believing that he would add greater overall strength to the faculty and would bring added respect from the medical community.

Both Dr. Willard's assumption and the misgivings of some others proved well founded. After he was appointed and had arrived in Lexington, Ben proceeded to recruit an impressive group of highly qualified academic surgeons and developed what from many perspectives was the College's strongest department. He also earned the respect and admiration of practicing surgeons in Lexington and throughout the State. Their pride in Ben Eiseman carried over to a pride in the College. At the same time Ben quickly revealed his fundamental disagreement with the concept of undifferentiated clinical services for adults and children, the concept of conjoint clinical teaching and the concept of a full full-time clinical faculty on which the Physicians' Services Plan was based. Thus, the College was faced with a dilemma. Not only was Ben resistant to some of the College's fundamental objectives, he was articulate, experienced, and persuasive and he seemed to enjoy thoroughly the role of devil's advocate. Ben brought to the conference table the same superb confidence in his own judgment that was so important for a surgeon in the operating room. Convinced that his positions were the right ones, he was resistant to compromise. When asked one day why he had come to Kentucky, disagreeing as he did with so many of the school's philosophical objectives, he grinned and said "because I came to change them."

COMMUNITY MEDICINE

In all of the studies that preceded the establishment of the

University of Kentucky Medical Center, there were references to the need to improve the health status of the people of the State, especially those in rural areas. The training of more physicians was seen as an essential, but not the only, step that was needed to address this issue. There was a need to make medical education available to rural youth and to stimulate their motivation to bring their services back to their home regions. There was a need to understand and appreciate the reciprocal relationships between the health status of people and the vitality of their communities. There was a need to know more about the health beliefs and values of Kentucky's people and how these affected their responses to illness and their utilization of health care resources. And there was a need to measure the resources themselves, identify gaps and work to fill these. As noted earlier, some of these issues were addressed by the planning staff for the medical center during the years before its activation. Considerations for culture, social structure and economy were incorporated into the selection and admission of medical students, the curriculum, the design of the hospital and planning for patient care.

These considerations also led to the establishment of a Department of Community Medicine within the College. In many respects community medicine represented an expansion of the traditional concept of public health and preventive medicine to provide a much broader and more intensive exposure of medical students to the health status, problems and resources of communities and their people. An ultimate goal of the program was to encourage students eventually to practice medicine in rural areas. In the second year students received a basic introduction to concepts of the distribution and determinants of disease in human populations including biostatistics, vital statistics, epidemiology, preventive medicine, community health organization, medical care financing and current trends in medical care. In the fourth year, after their basic clinical training, all students, on a rotating clerkship in community medicine, spent six weeks living in and "diagnosing" the health care status of a community. Sponsored by and working with a local physician and supervised by traveling "field professors" from the Department, students were expected to prepare an analysis of the health status of their communities, identify problems and suggest solutions. As an elective course, a few students each year had an opportunity to do an international clerkship studying communities with different cultural, social, economic and health characteristics.

The concept for Community Medicine was the brainchild of Kurt W. Deuschle. Deuschle had started his career in internal medicine, then moved to the field of public health and had developed a pioneering program of health care on a Navaho reservation. Willard was so impressed by Deuschle's philosophy and achievements that he moved him from an assistant professorship at Cornell to the rank of Professor and Chairman of Community Medicine at Kentucky. Community Medicine along with Behavioral Science became a symbol of innovation at Kentucky.

Kurt Deuschle's dedication and personal enthusiasm was "contagious." Students valued their field experiences and most even found excitement in the statistics of epidemiology. Several of the College's early graduates became disciples of Deuschle and went on to distinguished careers that built on their community medicine training and some of these became national leaders in health care policy and delivery.

Eventually, several members of Deuschle's department were recruited from Kentucky to develop the concept of community medicine at other medical schools. Therefore, when in 1968 Deuschle yielded to family pressures to return to the New York area, there was no logical successor at Kentucky. The Department struggled after Deuschle's departure and the program was eventually modified to a more traditional pattern.

STATE AND LOCAL SERVICES

Another expression of the value that the Medical Center and the College of Medicine placed on relating to the people and communities of Kentucky was the Division of State and Local Services, established in 1960. Directed by Robert L. Johnson, who had been trained at Yale in Public Health Administration, the Division was created to enable the College and the Center to give advice, support, and assistance to individuals, groups, agencies or communities engaged or interested in improving the health of Kentuckians. Johnson saw his program as somewhat analogous to the College of Agriculture's Extension Service. Although without county agents or home demonstration agents, the Division had a similar purpose of "bringing the resources and services of the University to the people of the State and working with them to achieve fuller lives." Activities of the Division included managing post-graduate education programs for health professionals, consulting with community development programs, working with community leaders interested in developing medical care facilities and services, working with the State Medical Association's Rural Health Council, and developing with the State Health Department professional education programs for local health officers. The Division also worked closely with the University's Public Relations Department and was initially responsible for medical center public information.

The resourcefulness of the concept of state and local services was called on in 1962 to help save the chain of hospitals in Eastern Kentucky and West Virginia that had been established by the Miners Memorial Hospital Association in 1956. Faced with a deficit in the Hospital's fund, the UMW announced that it would close them down. Bob Johnson, Bill Willard and Howard Bost were all involved in an effort to maintain this valuable source of care for an isolated and poverty stricken population. Eventually a combination of efforts saved the day. These included the national offices of the Presbyterian Church, the Federal government, and a $700,000 appropriation (to pay for services provided by the hospital system to persons unable to pay for their own care) that Governor Bert Combs obtained from a special session of the State legislature. Commenting on this effort in a 1964 article entitled "What a Medical School Can Be" the Louisville *Courier-Journal* noted that the College "is rapidly becoming recognized for the ability of its leadership. And under the guidance of Dean William R. Willard, services are by no means limited to teaching or research or to services merely to the Lexington area. Dr. Willard and his assistants were instrumental in bringing together the people, resources and view that finally saved the Miners Memorial Hospitals for Eastern Kentucky." (Feb. 1,1964)

During the early 1960s, Bill Willard, Howard Bost, Bob Johnson, Ed Pellegrino, Richard Segnitz (a pediatric surgeon) and others from the U.K. Medical Center played a major role in support of efforts to create a modern medical center in Morehead, Kentucky. The effort was spearheaded by Dr. C. Louise Caudill, a local obstetrician and family physician and supported by Adron Doran, President of Morehead State University, Monsignor Towell of the Covington diocese of the Roman Catholic Church and several community leaders in Rowan County. After nearly $300,000 had been raised locally, Howard Bost prepared an application for federal Hill-Burton funding through the State Health Department that made construction of a hospital possible. Throughout this complex process, Bob Johnson arranged for numerous meetings that brought together divergent interests and positions. Ed Pellegrino introduced the group to the Hunterdon model on which initial staff recruitment and organization were based, and Dick Segnitz provided both technical advice and encouragement. Bill Willard arranged to have the St. Claire Medical Center serve as a teaching hospital for the College of Medicine. Although many changes have occurred since its original conception, the St. Claire Medical Center has grown and served as a significant source of quality health care for Northeastern Kentucky. It has also served as a model for other outreach affiliations with the University of Kentucky. (For a detailed account of the transition of Morehead from a community with no hospital and scant medical resources to a major regional medical center, see James McConkey, *Rowan's Progress*, New York: Pantheon Press, 1992.)

MORE OUTREACH

In July of 1962, the first class of medical students began their third year with its series of rotations through clinical services. Because the University Hospital had been open only a few months and was still moving only gradually toward full activation, other sources of clinical training were needed. In anticipation of this need, Dr. Willard had negotiated with the Veterans Administration to provide a 100 bed general medical and surgical service at their large but previously strictly psychiatric hospital on Leestown Road, about five miles from the U.K. campus. Responsibility for the care of patients in these beds was vested in members of the clinical faculty from the College of Medicine and in V. A. physicians who qualified for faculty appointments. This arrangement was in essence a stop gap because negotiations were also underway for the Veterans Administration to construct a 400 bed teaching hospital adjacent to and corridor connected to the University Hospital. Following a pattern that has been established for so-called "Dean's Committee" V.A. teaching hospitals throughout the country, there are interlocking medical staff appointments between the College and the V.A., the Medical Director of the V.A. Hospital serves as an Assistant Dean in the College of Medicine and there are several additional shared or interchanged resources.

Affiliations were also arranged in 1962 with four Lexington hospitals - Cardinal Hill, Shriners, St. Joseph, and Good Samaritan, and with the United States Public Health Service Hospital - to provide additional selected clinical experiences.

From the earliest days of planning it was apparent that Lexington was already a center of medical care for the people from a fairly large region. While efforts would be made to avoid head-on competition with the other hospitals in the community, it was assumed that the University Hospital would have some skills and technology not available elsewhere and would serve as the referral "tertiary" hospital for patients who would be sent to Lexington from many parts of the State, especially the Eastern and Southern regions that were not being served by hospitals in Louisville or Cincinnati. In anticipation of this utilization, plans were made to construct a helicopter pad behind the medical center (approximately where the Department of Behavioral Science building now stands). The pad was actually built but rarely used in the 1960s and was eventually abandoned. The concept of patient transport

171

by helicopter was merely "ahead of its time." In the 1980s the University Hospital established an areomedical service that is among the best equipped and busiest in the country.

ACCREDITATION

From the earliest days of planning for the College of Medicine, an essential goal was that the College be fully accredited before the graduation of its first students. Responsibility for the accreditation of medical schools in the United States and Canada is vested in a Liaison Committee for Medical Education (LCME) comprised of representatives of the Association of American Medical Colleges and the American Medical Association. During the planning and developmental period, representatives of the LCME made three visits to Lexington. The first of these in September 1957 involved a review of the philosophy, the plans, the resources, the level of commitment by the state and university, and the qualifications of the staff. This resulted in an approval to proceed toward activation. The second visit was in October of 1961 when two classes of students were in progress. This involved reviews of the curriculum for the first two years, the qualifications of faculty members, the budget, and the plans for activating the hospital and initiating clinical instruction. The outcome of this review was positive with a recommendation of provisional accreditation. A third accreditation review was scheduled for April 1964, with the anticipation that its favorable findings would enable the first class of students to graduate from a fully accredited school.

As anticipated, the report of this third accreditation visit did indeed recommend full accreditation for the College. The report was complimentary on many criteria. It praised the facilities that had been provided for students (except noting that the study cubicles needed better noise reduction). It found the library "excellent." It noted that "much attention was given to the planning of the university hospital as a teaching hospital (with) ample facilities for the educational programs." It complimented the admission policies and procedures. The report gave particular attention to the curriculum that "has been built around the concept of graduating an undifferentiated physician and the general philosophy of comprehensive medicine." It expressed approval of the effort "to recognize the symbolic and concrete importance of certain aspects of the traditional organization and identification of the medical sciences and, at the same time, develop multi-discipline and correlated teaching whenever this seems logical and desirable." It selected for special mention the application of basic sciences to clinical medicine through the clinical-basic science conferences and other conjoint courses. It described the conjoint courses in detail and made special note of the innovative teaching of communication and interviewing, behavioral science and community medicine. "The team was impressed by the degree to which the Dean and the faculty are interested in and concerned about the problems of the community and the state and are trying to orient the educational program toward the understanding and solution of these problems."

The 1964 report called "successful" the effort to "combine individual departmental teaching efforts with conjoint teaching sessions." It praised the "new dimension in the breadth of medical student learning experience by incorporating the community as one of its active teaching areas." It concluded that the school "brought sufficient uniqueness and innovation to bear watching with predictable profit by the other medical education institutions of the country. The goal of excellence set by the university and the medical school and their active efforts to achieve it deserve praise."

Along with its high praise, the accreditation report of 1964 contained two messages of caution that proved to be prophetic. First, referring to changes in the administrative processes of the University that had been instituted by a new president, John Oswald, the report warned against superseding the authority of the dean. "Academic democracy must not be distorted to preclude the benefits of individual, responsible, creative leadership. ... The entire academic enterprise is weakened by administrative impotence in the deanship." Second, this report of April 1964 warned against a drift back toward traditionalism. "There is beginning evidence here and there of a return to traditional exercises at the sacrifice of some innovations that apparently had not yet actually been proved entirely unsatisfactory. It is hoped these changes are founded on careful evaluations of the merits for undergraduate medical education and not on traditional dependence upon curriculum hours as departmental status symbols or pure dislike or discomfort with things new and different."

AN ACHILLES' HEEL

In the early 1960s the College of Medicine appeared to have achieved a remarkable compatibility among its philosophical objectives, design of facilities, initial faculty recruitment, curriculum development, patient care planning, and physicians' services plan. There was also a sense of satisfaction with Dr. Willard's internal administrative style in which he delegated cleanly, invited full participation, listened well, and took personal responsibility for final decisions on major issues. For those who had come to know him and work with him, he inspired a fierce loyalty.

Yet, in retrospect, as the 1964 LCME report so insightfully identified, an Achilles' Heel was developing that would eventually have a significant impact on many of the College's unique features. Simply put, some of the Chairmen who were recruited by Dr. Willard and were attracted by his innovative vision and planning, did not recruit for their own departments people with the same philosophical convictions or commitment to change. Instead they seemed bent on creating discipline focused departments that would be well respected by their more traditionally oriented peers elsewhere. Also, the arrival of successive classes of students and the activation of the hospital created pressures to fill faculty positions as quickly as possible and traditionally oriented people were more plentiful and often more readily moveable. Changes in the budgeting for new faculty lines instituted by new University President Jack Oswald also had the effect of discouraging continuation of a deliberately orchestrated recruiting process. Following the activation of teaching and patient care programs, even in the recruitment of some of the department chairmen, there was less effort and success in assuring philosophical compatibility with and commitment to fundamental goals of the College than had gone into earlier recruiting. Gradually, over time, as the number of traditionally oriented faculty members increased, more traditional values seeped into discussions and eventually began to dominate decisions regarding the organization of curriculum and patient care and other innovative features of the College.

OTHER FACTORS OF CHANGE

Changes in the process of faculty recruitment and its gradual impact on the philosophical consensus of the faculty were by no means the only factors of change that were experienced by the college as it moved toward maturity. As in most institutions of higher education, severe space inadequacies rapidly became apparent. As more classes and faculty were added, the space allotted to college (and medical center) administration was far from adequate. With the availability of vastly increased funding for biomedical research in the 1960s, departments found that they had inadequate space to support their research funding potential. A new Department of Neurology (originally assumed to be a division of medicine) required offices and laboratories. And as the hospital moved toward full activation it became apparent that there were several functions for which no space or inadequate space had been allocated. With no provisions for adding to the medical center's buildings on the horizon, the College was faced with reallocating space from one function to another.

In a stroke of great fortune the College was able to persuade Dr. David B.Clark to move from his professorship at Johns Hopkins to develop and chair a Department of Neurology at Kentucky. David Clark was an outstanding clinician and teacher whose concern for and commitment to his patients was legendary. When one of my granddaughters was about two, she fell from a second story window. She was rushed to the U.K. Hospital's emergency room where Dr. Clark, alerted by my phone call, met her. After assuring himself that her injuries did not appear to be life-threatening, he suggested that she would be better off under observation at home rather than in the strange hospital setting.

However, at eleven in the evening Dr.Clark phoned to ask if we would "mind" if he came by to check up on the "wee lass." Sometime later, David was able to assure her parents that she would have no residual problems. Her father told her "Leigh, Dr. Clark says that you are going to be 'all right.' Whereupon, Leigh asked, "Daddy, will Dr. Clark be 'all right' too?" Leigh is now a medical student at the University of Kentucky.

The first victims of the space crunch were the students. First, a large section of study cubicles was displaced to make room for a Department of Neurology. The space occupied by the student lounge was diverted to administrative functions. The snack room also became offices. In response to pressure from more recently recruited faculty members, the space occupied by the students' unit laboratories and seminars was converted to departmental teaching or research labs. As the hospital moved toward full occupancy, many of the spaces that had been provided with special consideration for the social and psychological needs of patients and their families, and for improving communication, and demonstrating patient centered care were diverted to other needs.

During the same time frame, the curriculum was gradually modified toward a more traditional form. Many of the conjoint courses were turned over to departments. Communication and interviewing became the responsibility of behavioral science; human growth and development, initially taught by faculty from six departments, was assigned to psychiatry; conjoint science courses were assumed by newly established departments of pharmacology and cell biology. The conjoint third year clinical clerkships were unacceptable to the department of surgery. Within a few months they were modified into separate clerkships in medicine, surgery, pediatrics and psychiatry. The highly successful basic science-clinical conjoint conference was retained and the innovative courses in behavioral science and community medicine remained but the amount of collaborative teaching among faculty from two or more departments was reduced sharply.

Experiencing this period of retreat from innovation was painful. We apparently had not recruited enough medical educators with a spirit of adventure and a bent for innovation to out-weigh the forces of resistence to change. It was also painful to watch the impact of a new university administration on the abili-ty and eventually the will of Bill Willard to exert leadership and fight for his fundamental beliefs.

CHANGE OF COMMAND

In September 1962, Frank Dickey announced his resigna-tion as President of the University of Kentucky to be effective on July 1, 1963. During his seven years in office, Dickey had seen the Medical Center rise from its cornfield site and approach full activation. In addition, due to an infusion of funds for higher education that followed the institution of a State sales tax in 1960, the University had made a significant beginning toward upgrad-ing, renewing and expanding its physical resources and indeed rebuilding much of the central campus. As noted earlier, Frank Dickey had helped select and recruit Dr. Willard, and during his presidency he was trusting in his delegation of responsibility to Willard and supportive in according the latitude needed to create the Medical Center with all of its complexities.

Dickey's successor was John W. Oswald, a plant patholo-gist who had been the Vice President for Administration at the University of California in Berkeley. Jack Oswald brought with him to Lexington from Berkeley both a vision and an administra-tive style that were new to the University of Kentucky. In the words of historian Carl Cone "Oswald was in a hurry to push toward what seemed an attainable goal of greatness and the whole campus caught the sense of forward movement." At the same time, Cone noted, Oswald's approach was "heavy-handed" and caused "some unpleasantness." (Carl B. Cone, *The University of Kentucky, A Pictorial History*, Lexington: University Press of Kentucky, 1989.) Oswald won the approval of many faculty members by initiating a massive turnover of administrative per-sonnel. He also restructured administrative policies in ways that often reduced the authority while maintaining or increasing the responsibilities of administrators, especially deans and department chairs for whom he established rotating terms of office and a system of periodic review and evaluation. He also instituted rigorous procedures for the evaluation, promotion, and awarding of tenure for faculty and for determining salary increments. He transformed the faculty governance body into a University Faculty Senate and significantly enlarged its role in determining broad academic policies.

With the infusion of a significant increase in state funding for higher education, Oswald was able to add about 300 faculty lines to the University, promote a greater emphasis on research, increase support for graduate education, substantially increase faculty and staff benefits, institute a funded TIAA-CREF retirement system, and continue the massive building activity that had been initiated by the Dickey administration. After discovering that the University would become 100 years old in February of 1965, Oswald mobilized resources to assure an appropriate Centennial celebration that would bring recognition and respect to the University. In the words of Carl Cone, Oswald "brought an aggressive conviction that the vision of greatness was attainable."

Many of the people who applauded the choice of Jack Oswald as University President, saw in him a champion for "equalizing" the Medical Center and the rest of the University. For the majority of these, and they included most Medical Center personnel, this meant seeking the necessary resources to enable the whole University to achieve the standards of support for faculty, programs and buildings that had been obtained by the Medical Center. As noted in Chapter Three, this had long been the hope of the Medical Center's supporters in the University at large. However, for those who from the outset had feared the Medical Center's impact, opposed its establishment and fought to limit its development,"equalizing" meant reducing or eliminating the Medical Center's degree of freedom and limiting its further development.

According to Jack Oswald, he had discussed his coming to Kentucky with the presidents of a number of other universities and had been warned that medical centers meant problems for university presidents. Oswald had also come from a university system where the closest medical center was across the Bay in San Francisco and was an autonomous sister institution that competed with the Berkeley Campus for budget, resources and recognition.

The concept of presiding over a university that had accorded to the administrator of a subordinate unit the kind of latitude, essential to the Medical Center's development, that Bill Willard had obtained as Vice President of the University for the Medical Center and Dean of the College of Medicine, was inconsistent with Jack Oswald's administrative convictions and personal style.

Publicly, Jack Oswald had nothing but words of praise and respect for Bill Willard. He recognized that Willard was personally well liked and had earned widespread respect, trust and gratitude in the community, the state, the medical profession and the university. Oswald was generous in his references to Willard and his accomplishments. At the same time, within the University, many of Oswald's policies reduced Willard's ability to be effective.

Among Oswald's early administrative changes were an order prohibiting anyone outside of his office from contacting officials of State government without the approval of his office and a directive eliminating several features and policies that distinguished the Medical Center's budget from that of the rest of the University.

Much of the success in obtaining adequate state support for the Medical Center was due to the confidence and respect that Bill Willard and Howard Bost earned among the officials of State government with whom they dealt in Frankfort. Negotiations were not limited to finance and budgets and buildings but included regulations and legislation as well. Both Willard and Bost were knowledgeable and articulate. They were perceived as totally committed to the goals for which the Medical Center was founded and funded and as men of impeccable integrity. Carl Delabar, who had come from the State's Department of Finance to be the Medical Center's chief financial officer, was equally respected and trusted. Beyond the needs of the Medical Center, Willard, Bost and several faculty members of the College of Medicine were often asked to provide advice and leadership in numerous health related statewide endeavors. The edict that limited direct communication with state officials had an impact on the ability of Bill Willard and others in the Medical Center to participate and provide effective leadership in the development of health policy generally as well as represent the interests and needs of the University's health sector.

Internally, Oswald not only eliminated the Medical Center's separate budget, but he instituted restrictive modifications as well. These were to have a critical impact on faculty and staff recruitment. In the early 1960s, the Medical Center was experiencing rapid expansion. Each year brought new classes of students and with the activation of the hospital and clinics there were rapidly increasing numbers of patients. The pressure to serve more and more students and patients required a rapid acceleration in the recruitment of faculty, especially in the clinical departments. Although the State, responding to Governor Bert Combs' leadership, had provided solid support for operating the Medical Center, State funds were not adequate to meet the needs for rapid faculty expansion. As was the practice in other medical schools, it had been assumed from the beginning of planning that Kentucky's College of Medicine would rely significantly on fees from clinical service and on research and training grants for part of its operating budget. As the College and the hospital and clinics were activated, conservative projections of fee and grant income were used as a basis for authorizing recruiting. In addition, in recognition of the fact that recruitment would move more rapidly in some areas than others, and in order to avoid freezing recruitment funds where they would not be used, funds for recruiting new personnel were pooled and allotted to whichever departments were able to recruit the best people.

Oswald imposed two significant restrictions on this process. First, he insisted that the budget identify specific positions to be filled with specific salaries for each position. This removed the option of using funds flexibly in order to recruit the best qualified people. Oswald further restricted flexibility by eliminating the inclusion of projected income from fees and grants in the budget construction. These changes made it difficult for the

College to recruit enough new faculty members to keep pace with increasing numbers of students and patients. This also had the effect of compromising the careful recruiting process that Dr. Willard had established. Desperate for help, departments tended to use their faculty lines to recruit the first technically qualified people they could find, without considering the candidates' philosophical compatibility with the mission and goals of the College or their interest in meeting the particular needs of Kentucky. By the mid 1960s an increasing number of faculty of the College had never even heard of the Statement of Philosophy and looked upon the innovative features of curriculum and patient care as targets for change so that they could get on to doing things as they had been done in the traditional schools from which they had come.

Within the University, President Oswald sought to redefine Dr. Willard's responsibilities so that he would function as a Vice President of the total University, not just for the Medical Center. He added to Willard's job some time consuming university-wide tasks that had the effect of making Willard Oswald's assistant. Oswald also assumed some roles that had been Willard's. For example, whereas Frank Dickey had made sure that it was Dr. Willard who reported about Medical Center developments to the Board of Trustees, State agencies such as the Council on Higher Education, and the general public, Jack Oswald usually assumed this role himself.

Additionally, President Oswald decreed that the tasks of Vice President and Dean of the College of Medicine were too much for one individual and, in 1964, he appointed a committee to recommend that these offices be separated and a new Dean recruited for the College. By his various actions, President Oswald created a self-fulling prophecy. It was probably true that (as the 1964 College accreditation team had observed), a year into the Oswald administration, Dr. Willard's effectiveness as the College of Medicine's Dean had been diminished. There were now many types of decisions that he was no longer authorized to make and act on without the review of committees and the approval of higher authority. Perhaps most significant was the frustration and the personal difficulty that Willard was experienc-

181

ing in dealing with the severe restrictions that were imposed on his administrative authority.

Despite my close personal friendship with and loyalty to Bill Willard, I had to agree that by 1964, he was no longer functioning as effectively as he once had in his role as Dean. A man who for years had worked 18 hour days and maintained his sharpness and sparkle was now showing signs of fatigue and frustration.

It is my personal belief that because Jack Oswald had imposed conditions that prevented Bill Willard from continuing to perform effectively in the role of Dean and Vice-President, Bill was increasingly responsive to requests to serve elsewhere. These activities involved a great deal of travel and they took him away from frustrating and unpleasant situations in Lexington and provided him with a sense of reward and satisfaction for jobs well done that he could no longer count on experiencing at the University of Kentucky.

He was much sought after as a consultant and he began to accept more and more requests to share his own experience and wisdom with others. He served as a consultant to ten of the new medical schools that were being developed at the time. In 1962, he had been appointed by President Kennedy as Chairman of a Health Resources Advisory Committee to the Executive Office of the President, a position he was to hold through the Johnson administration as well. By 1964 he was serving on key committees and chairing several of these for the American Medical Association, the Association of American Medical Colleges, the National Board of Medical Examiners, the American Public Health Association, the United States Public Health Service, the W. K. Kellogg Foundation, the Council of Medical Administrators, and these were just the national groups and did not include numerous regional and state activities.

As chairman of the Council on Medical Education of the American Medical Association's Committee on Education for Family Practice, he authored the so-called "Willard Report" entitled "Meeting the Challenge of Family Practice." This report had a profound influence on medical education by establishing the basis for the acceptance of family practice as a recognized specialty, suggesting criteria for the certification of family practice specialists and leading to the creation of departments of family practice in many medical schools, including Kentucky.

I don't believe that Jack Oswald felt any personal animosity towards Bill Willard. On the contrary, he admired him. However, Oswald was personally ambitious and he brought to the University of Kentucky an administrative culture and style that was in direct conflict with Willard's. As time went on, Oswald and his family were patients of several of the College's clinical chiefs and Oswald encouraged them to "report" directly to him about the administration of the College of Medicine. Thus, in several respects, the concerns expressed by the 1964 accreditation team about the impact of Oswald's administrative style and policies on the College of Medicine and its Dean were indeed prophetic.

There were several ironies in the search for a new Dean of the College of Medicine. Nearly all of the department chairmen in the College of Medicine and most of the early faculty recruits said that the primary attraction that brought them to Lexington had been Bill Willard, both the man and his philosophy. They had come to work with and for Bill Willard and they really did not want another Dean. Jack Greene, Willard's choice in 1962 to chair Obstetrics and Gynecology, has expressed his own feelings. He recalls Bill Willard as a man of "total dedication," who made "great contributions to medical education, related to people in a most considerate way" and was "one of the greatest men I've ever known" (personal communication). Such respect was shared by the faculty members who were appointed by Oswald to serve as a search committee. Furthermore, most of the medical educators who might have been applicants for the position were either friends or admirers of Bill Willard. It was no secret that he had been reluctant to give up the Deanship or that the faculty were reluctant to have him do so. Faced with these realities and their own assessment of the administrative arrangement, many of the potential candidates who were approached about the job declined to be considered. Others who visited Lexington withdrew after they had evaluated the situation. It took nearly three years before

Dr. William S. Jordan, Jr., Chairman of the Department of Public Health and Preventive Medicine at the University of Virginia, was persuaded to take on the unenviable task of succeeding Bill Willard as Dean.

Until 1964, the offices of Dean of the College of Medicine and Vice President for the Medical Center had been run jointly. Not only did Dr. Willard hold both positions, but they shared the same physical space and most of his support staff had responsibilities that involved both the college and the medical center. When it became apparent that the search process would be prolonged, Dr. Thomas Whayne, a retired Public Health officer who had joined Dr. Willard's staff, was asked to assume some of the Dean functions on an acting basis. Dr. Willard eventually moved his Vice President's office to a former motel across Rose Street from the Medical Center in order to provide space, a physical separation and an independent identity for the College of Medicine's administration. One of the first tasks that Bill Jordan faced when he arrived as Dean in 1967 was to develop a free standing administrative structure for the College. At the same time, Jordan was faced with recruiting replacements for several of the original department chairmen, winning the confidence of the faculty and their responsiveness to his own administrative style and adapting to the University's and Medical Center's structure and bureaucracy.

Bill Willard's departure from the Dean's office and Bill Jordan's arrival symbolized a transition for the College of Medicine. Having survived its birth and infancy it was now poised for its developmental years. For a number of the faculty leaders, the change of Deans provides a logical transition as well.

SOME KEY PEOPLE LEAVE, AND SOME REMAIN

As noted by both Frank Dickey and Julius Richmond in their tributes to Bill Willard, one of Willard's strengths was his ability to identify and attract to work with him people who themselves had potential capacities for leadership. Not surprisingly, within a short time, many of Willard's early recruits for Kentucky were being invited to consider positions elsewhere. Although some whose roots in the institution and the community became firmly established chose to remain in Lexington, by the mid-1960s the College had lost a number of those who played key roles in its development.

The first to go was Alan Ross who in 1962 was recruited by Johns Hopkins University where he soon became Chairman of the Department of Statistics in the School of Hygiene and Public Health. The Rosses' decision to leave Lexington was motivated partly by the availability in Baltimore of appropriate schooling for their son who was blind.

Alfred Brandon, who had so effectively created from scratch a remarkably complete and valuable medical library, followed Ross to Johns Hopkins. Brandon's miracle at Kentucky attracted national attention and in 1962 he was invited to become Director of the William Welch Medical Library.

Richardson Noback was the second member of the planning staff to leave. Dick became the founding Dean of a new medical school established by the University of Missouri in Kansas City.

Robert Johnson was initially recruited to a different position within the University of Kentucky. John Oswald, who succeeded Frank Dickey as University President in 1963, was impressed by Johnson's effectiveness in developing the Medical Center's program of services to the state and local communities, recognized Johnson's considerable talents for innovation and administration. Johnson became a Vice President in the Oswald administration. Later, Bob would serve as Vice President of the University of California, become the founding Director of a national health information organization, and subsequently would return to Kentucky as President of the Appalachian Regional Hospitals (now Appalachian Regional Healthcare).

Among the basic science chairs, Bill Knisely was the first to break ranks. Bill left Lexington to become the Director of a newly formed Institute of Biology and Medicine with responsibility for coordinating the development of a new medical school at

Michigan State University. Bill would later become Vice Chancellor for Health Affairs in the University of Texas System and President of the Medical College of South Carolina before closing out his career at the University of Oklahoma.

In 1966, Loren Carlson was recruited by the University of California in Davis to head the development of the basic science division in their newly established medical school. Loren's research on space medicine while at Kentucky would later be recognized as basic to the development of the national space program.

For several years, Ed Pellegrino resisted a constant barrage of invitations to consider other positions of leadership in academic medicine. Finally, in 1966 he was enticed away by the State University of New York to lead the development of a new medical center at their Stoney Brook campus. As noted in Chapter Five, this was the first of a series of academic leadership positions that Pellegrino would hold throughout his distinguished career.

Richard Wittrup, after seeing the University Hospital achieve full activation, accepted the challenge of managing and eventually directing the merger of several of the Harvard affiliated hospitals in Boston.

Roy Jarecky was recruited to join the staff of the Association of American Medical Colleges but, after two years in Washington, was drawn back to the College of Medicine where he would hold several administrative positions before eventually retiring in Lexington.

Not all departures were motivated by the lure of positions of greater responsibility. Jack Githens, who had been torn about leaving Colorado when he accepted the chairmanship in Pediatrics, decided after just four years in Lexington to return to the ski slopes and his former department at the University of Colorado. In 1966, Ben Eiseman followed Githens back to the ski slopes and medical community of Colorado. As already noted, Ben had been a spectacular recruiter. At least eight of the men who Eiseman brought to the Department of Surgery at Kentucky, including Ward Griffen who succeeded him, eventually became chairmen of their own surgery departments.

In 1968, Kurt Deuschle, who created at Kentucky the first Department of Community Medicine in a medical school, left Lexington for family reasons and returned to New York City where he transferred his model of community medicine to a new department that he founded and chaired at the Mount Sinai School of Medicine. A year later, Joe Parker returned to Duke.

Not all those who were beckoned chose to leave the University of Kentucky or Lexington. Howard Bost and Robert Straus, like Bill Willard, were drawn into numerous temporary assignments in both Frankfort and Washington. Bost, who had authored Kentucky's medical assistance program, was asked to help draft the federal medicaid and medicare legislation (and invited by President Johnson to witness its signing). He then took a year's leave of absence to serve as Deputy Director in the Bureau of Health Insurance of the Social Security Administration where he helped draft regulations for administering the programs. In the 1960s Straus was recruited to help write guidelines for the national community mental health program. He later chaired two national study commissions in the field of alcoholism, recommendations from which were incorporated in legislation establishing the National Institute on Alcohol Abuse and Alcoholism. Both Bost and Straus would be continually involved in state and national health related activities throughout their careers but both would elect to maintain their primary roles at Kentucky as Vice Chancellor the Medical Center (Bost) and as Chairman of Behavioral Science in the College of Medicine (Straus).

Carl Delabar, was recruited to be Director of Finance, remained with the Medical Center through the rest of his career. Of the first basic science chairmen, George Schwert, after developing a very strong Department of Biochemistry, relinquished the chair but remained as one of the College's outstanding teachers until he too reached retirement age. Harold Rosenbaum who developed and chaired the Department of Radiology and John W. Greene, chairman of Obstetrics and Gynecology both would elect to remain in Lexington providing distinction and stability for their respective Departments.

After turning the office of Dean of the College of

Medicine over to Dr. William S. Jordan, Jr. in 1967, Bill Willard continued to serve as Vice President for the Medical Center until the fall of 1970. From then, until his retirement in 1972, he served as Special Assistant for Health Affairs to University President Otis Singletary. Dr. Willard was succeeded as Vice President by Peter P. Bosomworth. Peter had come to Kentucky as chairman of the Department of Anesthesiology in 1962. He had developed a strong and highly respected department and had also served as Associate Dean of Clinical Affairs for the College and, briefly, as Acting Director for the University Hospital.

For at least two years prior to leaving Kentucky, Bill Willard had been seeking a retirement avocation and had become interested in catfish farming. He found a catfish farm for sale in Moundville, Alabama and arranged to purchase it. However, even before he and Adalyn could complete their move, word of his coming to Alabama spread and he was recruited to become the founding Dean of another new health professional school. This was a two-year program located at the University of Alabama in Tuscaloosa. Unlike most previous two-year medical schools this one covered the 3rd and 4th years, providing the clinical years of medical education for students who had completed the first two years in the basic sciences at the State's medical campus in Birmingham. The new school was called College of Community Health Sciences and the training was focused on primary care aimed at preparing physicians who would be committed to begin their medical practice in areas of need in Alabama. As he had done at Kentucky, Willard included a significant role for the behavioral sciences in both the planning for and the implementation of this new college. He also emphasized the role of the college as a community resource and the role of communities in the training of physicians.

After successfully launching one more innovative medical school, Bill Willard retired again in 1979. As long as his health permitted, he continued to be sought and to provide national service as a consultant on issues of medical education and health care delivery.

Shortly after his retirement from Kentucky, Bill Willard

was selected by the Association of American Medical Colleges to be the recipient of its highest honor, the Abraham Flexner Award. At various times, he was also the recipient of awards for distinguished service from the American Medical Association, the American Board of Family Practice, the Kentucky Medical Association and the Kentucky Public Health Association. He was also awarded honorary degrees by four universities including the University of Kentucky and Transylvania.

Bill Willard died in 1992 at the age of 84.

RECAPITULATION

In keeping with their perception of the expectations of those who made it possible for the University of Kentucky to develop a College of Medicine, Dr. Willard and his associates had tried to create a "new" kind of medical school. They envisioned a school that would acknowledge that the primary reasons for its existence were to meet the educational and developmental needs of its students; to advance medical knowledge; to demonstrate exemplary patient care; and to extend its resources and services to help improve the health of the people of Kentucky at the community level, in rural as well as urban settings. In order to meet these goals, they recruited an initial group of colleagues who shared these philosophical objectives, were attracted by innovation, and felt secure in departing from tradition.

If the findings of the LCME accreditation team that visited the College in 1964 can be accepted as an objective evaluation, the College did indeed begin with unique provisions for its students, an innovative curriculum, an effort to meet the social and psychological as well as the purely biological needs of its patients, and a substantial investment in extending its impact out into the communities of Kentucky. However, the accreditation team also noted the beginnings of a "drift toward traditionalism" and they expressed concern that changes in the administrative structure of the University were causing "administrative impotence" in the leadership.

In May, 1975, Dr. William R. Willard, the Dean of the

College of Community Health Sciences of the University of Alabama, delivered an address entitled "A 'New Generation' Medical School" before a conference on Undergraduate Medical Education in Family Practice in Kansas City. In this address, Willard cast his creation at the University of Kentucky with what he termed the newer "old generation" schools. He noted that "old generation" schools had not lacked for innovation, citing particularly the introduction of the social and behavioral sciences and of community medicine, improved teaching methods, curriculum experimentation, and changes in the selection and nurturing of students. He noted that the newer "old generation" schools had started "with vision and enthusiasm to make medical education different and better than it was elsewhere and more relevant to the needs of society." After mentioning the requisite heavy involvement in "bricks and mortar," in raising money and the myriad details of planning and developing the school, Willard noted that "faculty had to be recruited rapidly, and about the only place to go for them was to established medical schools. Hence, new faculty arrived with their traditional ideas and values, followed quickly by students. Before one could realize it, the new school was cast in the traditional mold."

Willard went on to note that medical schools as social institutions must be responsive to public pressures, demands and expectations as reflected by governmental appropriations and that during the quarter century following World War II there was a public assumption that if we could do enough biomedical research and train enough physicians we could solve virtually all of the country's health needs. These expectations dictated sources of funding. The need for medical schools to go "where the money was" was too powerful to be overcome by those, like the Kentuckyplanning group, who were trying to anticipate the future. Thus, in hindsight, Bill Willard concluded that Kentucky's College of Medicine was molded less by its planning objectives than by the combination of public expectations, sources of available funding, and by the reality that a majority of available faculty members were motivated more by their traditional backgrounds than by a future orientation or an interest in innovation. Ever the gentleman, Bill Willard omitted reference to the changes in university administration that had curtailed his leadership at Kentucky at a critical time in the implementation of innovations.

As the decade of the 1970s began, Kentucky's College of Medicine had become more like most other medical schools. This is not to suggest that it became less strong. According to the criteria by which most medical schools were judged at the time, Kentucky became much stronger. Some of its innovations such as behavioral science and community medicine were widely emulated. At the same time, as Bill Willard noted in his 1975 address, many changes - scientific, political and economic - that had not been anticipated by the planning process, were beginning to impinge significantly on medical education and higher education both nationally and in Kentucky. Some of these changes will be considered briefly in Chapter Seven along with some comments on the status of the college today.

Lowering the boom. The "boomerangs" statue being lowered into its first home in the middle of a fountain in front of the hospital.

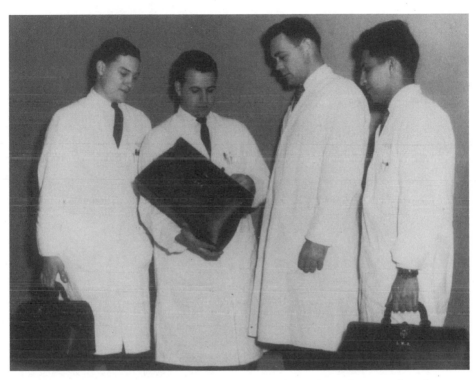

Symbols of success. First year students of the first class, Richard Geist, Martin Gebrow, Tom Hagan and S. Alavi examine their doctor's bags.

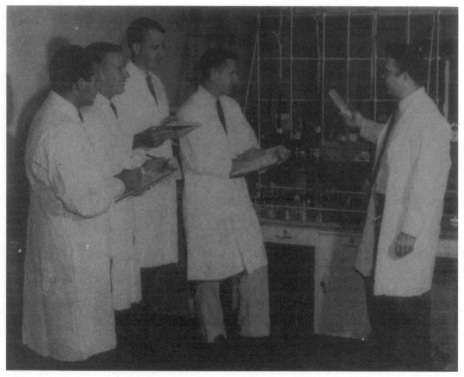

Student laboratories. Biochemist Robert Blitz brings instruction to students Martin Gebrow, Troy Burchett, Joe Christian and William Markesbery in the students' own laboratory.

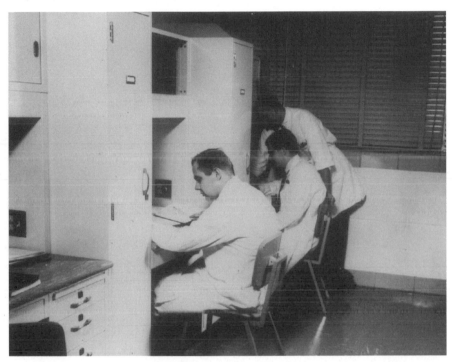

Student studies. Each student has a personal desk and locker area demonstrated here by Joseph Biggs, James Cunningham and Ballard Wright.

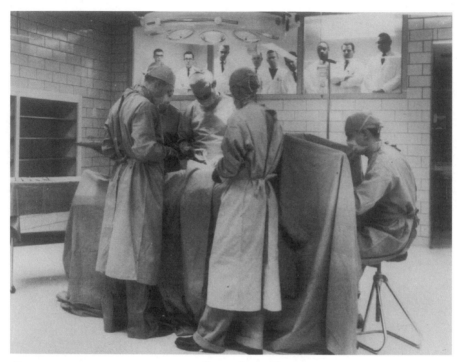

Supervising surgery. Nine students from the Class of 1964 are shown watching a surgical procedure from a special observation room. Within a few years, closed circuit television would enable students to have a bird's eye view.

*Student Claude Farley and behavioral scientist Robert Straus
demonstrate the use of one way glass in a class on communicating
and interviewing. This was a short-lived innovation soon to be sup-
planted by closed circuit television.*

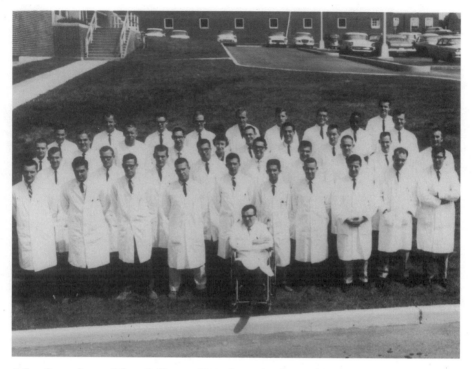

The first class. The College of Medicine's class of 1964.

Richard Haines' "Science of Man" murals, the fountain and Amarigo Brioschi's "boomerangs" sculpture before they were moved to make way for the first expansion of the hospital.

Flying doctors. With the completion of the hospital, a helicopter pad was located in a field just behind the Medical Center. Primitive in comparison with today's aeromedical service, the pad was "ahead of its time."

The Medical Center as viewed from Rose Street shortly after the opening of the University Hospital in 1962.

The first Professor and Chairman of Internal Medicine, Edmund D. Pellegrino.

Chapter Seven

MEETING THE
CHALLENGE OF CHANGE

Writing in 1969 for his own (Harvard) medical alumni magazine, Dr. William S. Jordan, Jr., the College of Medicine's second dean, noted that the school was no longer in its infancy, but approaching adolescence. He pointed out that by the time the College had graduated its fifth class in 1968 the faculty had already revised the original curriculum. While proud of its contributions to behavioral science and community medicine, it was "painfully conscious of its failure to design meaningful programs for comprehensive care," and "despite an expressed commitment to the philosophy of family practice, the first attempt to develop a residency program in family practice failed." Apart from behavioral science and community medicine, Jordan characterized other departments of the College as "conventional." He suggested that this may have occurred because in a new school the faculty felt insecure in their identity among their disciplinary peers nationally and, therefore, were more inclined to emulate established models than to be innovative or experimental themselves. Jordan went on to note that the school had "a faculty of competent men whose growing programs are overflowing a handsome building considered more than adequate just 10 year ago. The Dean's space cupboard, like his purse is bare."

Bill Jordan's references to his "space cupboard" and his "purse" described a situation that was not at all unique to the University of Kentucky's College of Medicine. Medical schools throughout the United States were experiencing similar pressures on their space and their budgets resulting from externally induced growing pains and challenges from unanticipated factors of change.

One such factor was a steep escalation in federal appropriations for research. Science was riding a crest of popular public support. In medicine it was assumed that no disease could not be prevented or cured if enough money was spent on research. Expanded opportunities for research funding led to the rapid expansion of medical school faculties. Research productivity, more than teaching excellence, became the major criterion in faculty evaluation. At Kentucky, most of the basic science departments began to attract significant research grant support, and quite quickly the numbers of people they employed as faculty and staff exceeded the planning projections and the allocated space. In the late 1960s, detailed plans were drawn for the addition of two floors to the basic science building but, with the Medical Center just recently completed, the project was low on the University's and the State's priority lists for new construction. The College had to be content with acquiring some additional research laboratories in two low-cost temporary buildings. (It would be about 25 years before the State would help fund the construction of a new state-of-the-art facility for biomedical research.)

A byproduct of research was the development of new technology that altered the process of patient care for many diseases and the kinds of equipment and facilities required to treat them. The implementation of new technology required ever increasing amounts of both space and money that were far beyond the projections that had been made during the College's planning process.

During this same period, the nation as well as Kentucky was experiencing a perceived shortage of physicians and there was pressure on all medical schools to increase the size of their student bodies beyond the capacity for which they had been designed. With the incentive of a Federal capitation grant, Kentucky stretched its entering class, admitting 108 students to facilities that had been designed for a maximum of 80 (only to drop the class size back to 95 a few years later when it was later assumed by the Council on Higher Education that the State might be training too many physicians).

Another national issue that arose at this time was that of preparing medical students for the practice of family medicine. Although the College had been created with a general commitment to train physicians for primary care, there was no formal provision for teaching family practice as a discrete specialty in the organization of the faculty or the curriculum. It was assumed that, in accordance with the school's philosophy, the clinical departments would orient their teaching toward primary care. However, as more and more traditionally oriented faculty members and clinical specialists were recruited, clinical teaching was becoming increasingly specialty oriented and moving away from a strong emphasis on primary care.

Stimulated by the A.M.A.'s "Willard Report," that led to the creation of a specialty board in family practice and provided an impetus for the creation of departments of family practice in many medical schools throughout the country, the Kentucky legislature in 1971 mandated the creation of such departments at the Universities of Louisville and Kentucky. Thereupon, the University of Kentucky Board of Trustees, honored Bill Willard by voting to establish the William R. Willard Department of Family Practice within the College of Medicine.

Ironically, although the Department of Family Practice was well received by a significant number of Kentucky's students, it was not eagerly received by most of the clinical faculty who saw it as competing for funds, students, patients and space. They expressed concern that family practice lacked a discipline and a research base and they tended to denigrate the quality of its training. Because the available clinic space and hospital beds were already committed to the specialty departments, a small building (named for Brick Chambers) was created to house the Department of Family Practice. However, it was located across Rose Street from the rest of the College and the Family Practice faculty cared for their patients who needed hospitalization at Central Baptist Hospital. Thus, in its inception, the Department of Family Practice did not become well integrated into either the educational or clinical activities of the College.

Ironically also, despite Bill Jordan's background in public health and expressions of enthusiastic support for Kurt Deuschle's programs in Community Medicine, after Deuschle moved on in 1968, Jordan failed to recruit a successor with a similar orientation. Soon, what had been one of the College's strongest and most innovative programs was focusing primarily on infectious diseases and more traditional aspects of preventive medicine.

THE CHANGING ECONOMIC BASE OF ACADEMIC MEDICINE

Beginning in the mid-1960s (and continuing in the 1990s) the nation has experienced radical changes in the economics of health care that have had a heavy impact on medical education. With the passage of Medicare and Medicaid legislation by the Congress in 1966, the provisions therein for honoring "usual and customary" charges for professional services set off a rapid escalation in the potential income of physicians that far exceeded the inflationary trends of the society as a whole. With this, the gap between the income potential of academic physicians and that of their colleagues in private practice began to get wider. This brought pressures to increase substantially the salaries of academic physicians, pressures that far exceeded the resources in most medical school budgets. Within the College of Medicine, salary schedules that were quite acceptable, in the early 1960s when most of the original clinical faculty were recruited, were no longer competitive by the end of the decade, especially in the higher income producing specialties. Pressures mounted within the clinical faculty to modify the "full full-time" concept in order to provide more income for physicians, recognize the differential in earning capacities of specialities and individuals, and give clinical faculty members some control over the allocation of income from fees for their services. Resistence to such changes came from most basic science faculty and from those among the clinical faculty and administration who valued the opportunity to teach, do research and care for patients in an academic setting sheltered from competitive pressures to maximize their income. However, the disparity between academic salaries and the income of physicians in private practice continued to grow. Initially, a compromise was reached that retained the structure of the Physicians Services Plan while providing for bonuses for clinical faculty in accordance with their income productivity. However, the issues were far from resolved.

In late 1973, Bill Jordan decided to forego academic administration in favor of a position with the National Institutes of Health. The unresolved issues noted above were inherited by his successor, D. Kay Clawson, who was recruited from his position as Chairman of the Department of Orthopedics at the University of Washington to be the College of Medicine's third Dean.

By the time that Kay Clawson arrived in 1975, the "full full-time" arrangement for hiring and compensating clinical faculty that had seemed so attractive when the College of Medicine was established was under continuing fire and, indeed, such plans were being abandoned by medical schools all over the country. Neither state support for public medical schools nor endowments and philanthropy for private schools could keep up with the sharply rising demands on medical school budgets to increase the compensation for their clinical faculty members to more closely approximate the earning potential of their counterparts in private practice. In Kentucky, as elsewhere, the incomes of physicians were escalating rapidly, creating gaps of as much as 100 or even 200 percent or more (depending on the field of specialty and the community) between the prevailing salaries of academic physicians and their income potential if they were in private practice.

The College was increasingly threatened with a loss of clinical faculty either to private practice or to medical schools that had found a way to make their compensation more competitive with the private sector. After months of agonizing, a plan for establishing the Kentucky Medical Services Foundation (KMSF) emerged. This created a non-profit corporation to manage the billing and collection of fees for clinical services provided by College of Medicine clinicians and to distribute the proceeds according to formulas contained in plans developed by each clinical department under contractual agreements with the University. As with the old PSP, a certain proportion of the funds collected by the KMSF was allocated to the Medical Center and the College of Medicine to offset overhead costs and provide for some academic enrichment. However, under the KMSF control of the funds was vested in the clinical faculty rather than the College and University. The net effect of the shift to the KMSF plan was to remove limits imposed by the College's budget on the potential income of clinician faculty members. Although formally subject to the Dean's approval, these would be determined within each department according to the department's plan for distribution of income from clinical services. At the same time, the amount of money contributed by the University from State appropriated funds, and guaranteed by tenure when it was awarded, was set at fixed limits according to rank. Thus, for a clinical faculty member, whatever his or her total compensation might be, the amount received from College resources and guaranteed by tenure would be fixed at from $22,000 to $40,000, depending on academic rank.

This major change in medical school financing was not accomplished easily or without cost. Initially, the change was again opposed by most basic science faculty who feared that with their income tied to the volume of patient care they provided, clinical faculty members would shift more of their time and effort to patient care at the expense of their participation in teaching, research and academic service. The KMSF plan was also opposed by some clinicians, particularly those who felt that large discrepancies in income among faculty were not appropriate for academic medicine, and who shared the concern of the basic scientists that teaching, service and research would suffer.

During the months of discussion that led to the creation of the KMSF, considerations of financing preempted discussions about education and patient care at the lunch table and in department meetings. There were many long evening meetings in private homes and several "white papers" were written. Most of the members of the Department of Psychiatry and several individuals from other clinical departments opted to remain within the PSP, an option that was soon phased out. At Kentucky and nationally, while justified as a means of survival for medical schools, the shift away from "full full-time" has altered the "culture" of medical schools. A symbolic example of such change was reflected in the conversation at the lunch tables. In the early years of the College, discussions at lunch almost always were concerned with educational or philosophical issues or with patient care. Eating with colleagues from different departments provided an opportunity to share their perspectives. After the issue of clinician incomes became so dominant, lunch table conversation became increasingly restricted to money, benefits and material things.

As the years passed, with a steady rise in the College of Medicine's total budget, the percentage supported by State dollars decreased steadily (from over 90 percent when the College was established to less than 20 percent in the mid-1990s). Dependence on funds generated by the clinical services of the faculty and the hospital increased accordingly, becoming the major source of operating funding for the clinical departments. They have contributed substantially to the support of other educational and research functions of the College. They have also been a major source of financing for additions to the outpatient facilities known as the Kentucky Clinic and they have helped pay for numerous other additions or alterations to the College of Medicine's physical plant.

The clinical departments have not been alone in feeling pressure to generate their own support. Although the full salaries of basic science faculty members in tenure track lines are provided from the state appropriation to the University, most other functions of these departments have become dependent on funds generated by research grants or contracts. Once considered a source of enrichment, funds from grants and contracts are as much a necessity for the operation of basic science departments as fees from patient care are for clinical departments. A fundamental difference is that the salaries of basic science tenure track faculty are not yet dependent on the amount of outside money that their research activities generate (although some of the private medical schools are moving in this direction).

Research and other scholarly productivity, most of which depends on outside funding, is, however, a major criterion in faculty evaluation and on the awarding of promotion and tenure. With pressures in clinical departments restricting opportunities for research and pressures on all departments competing with teaching for faculty time, many departments turned to the University's provision for a "special title," (non-research) faculty series. Special title appointments are often used for gifted teachers who, as long as they maintain their scholarship, can receive tenure and promotions without meeting the regular title expectations for research based publications. In addition, clinical departments began to rely on the special title series to appoint members who would be expected to carry a particularly heavy load of patient care. More recently, clinical departments have added a "clinical series" for appointments that carry the major expectation of patient care but no tenure or other long range commitments. The College also added a "research series" for the appointment of investigators who are tied to specific, time limited research projects and have no other major responsibilities. The increasing resort to special title, clinical and research series for faculty appointments reflects in part an effort to generate the increasing volume of income from patient care and research that is essential in order to support the College's basic educational mission while freeing more of the time of the regular titled faculty to participate in fulfilling this mission.

As the pressure to attract outside funding for research has mounted and the funding from federal sources has plateaued and seems destined to be cut, Universities have increasingly turned to a partnership with industry as an additional source of research support. Of major concern with both federal and industrial funding in the 1990s is the fact that there are fewer opportunities to obtain research support for ideas and projects that are investigator driven rather than those that meet politically motivated administrative priorities of the federal government or commercially motivated priorities of industry. This raises issues that are philosophical and political as well as economic and have national significance that goes far beyond medical education or a particular College of Medicine.

The experience of the University of Kentucky College of Medicine in trying to fulfill its basic missions and retain its goals and purpose in the face of ever increasing pressures to be self-supporting is but one small example of the contradictions of purpose that characterize health care in the United States. The future of health care seems destined for as yet uncharted change, and the only certainty is that the College of Medicine will be facing continuing change, whatever it may be. Having reviewed some of the economic imperatives to which the College has had to adapt, it is now fitting to consider how the College has fulfilled its original philosophical objectives, and to what extent it has fulfilled its commitment to the concepts of patient centered care, student centered education, integration with the University, and reaching out to the people and the communites of the State.

PATIENT CENTERED CARE

The original philosophy of medical education (Chapter Four) on which planning for the College of Medicine was based, stressed the importance of providing for students demonstrations of exemplary patient care. As noted in Chapter Six, planning for the University Hospital included many provisions that were designed to ease the experience of patients and their families, teach by example appropriate ways of communicating with and about patients, and consider the total experience of the patient, not just their medical intervention. Although there were many in the medical and hospital community who saw the University Hospital as an opportunity to "dump" their indigent patients, the goals of medical education also required that the patient population represent the general population both in terms of their health and medical status and their social and demographic characteristics. The growing need for the College and the Hospital to be "self-supporting" in order to maintain their financial integrity added still another reason why the College needed to meet its initial objective of attracting a patient population that would represent a broad spectrum of the general population and would include those who were well insured and financially solvent as well as the medically indigent.

In the mid-1970s, at Dean Kay Clausen's initiative, the College, with the Hospital, set out to examine its commitment to patient centered care and its teaching model with the goal of improving the experiences of hospitalized patients. A study was designed to identify deficiencies in the total experience of patients, and the third floor of the North wing of the Hospital was made available for establishing and testing ways of modifying the patient experience. To plan and oversee this project, Kay Clawson appointed a 3-North committee that included the chiefs of the clinical services and representatives from nursing, social work, hospital administration and behavioral science. After a study that included following a number of patients throughout their entire hospital experiences from their admission to their discharge, and interviewing many more patients as well as hospital personnel, the committee developed a program of "patient centered care" to be instituted on a remodeled 3-North unit. Features of the 3-North program included a provision for communicating with patients prior to admission (explaining where and when to come and inviting their questions), and a provision for personally escorting patients through the admission process. Training was provided for 3-North personnel about the various diagnostic and treatment procedures that patients experience so that they could explain these to their patients ahead of time and the patients would know what to expect. Patient transportation was scheduled to eliminate avoidable waiting. The number of hospital personnel with whom patients would have contact was reduced and a primary nurse was provided to coordinate and have responsibility for the entire patient experience. Patients were provided with a rapid follow-up of information following procedures. The unit was designed to provide a more homelike atmosphere with flexibility regarding when patients had to be in bed, use of their own clothing, the timing and content of meals, arrangements for visitors, and other efforts to adapt to the patient's rather than the hospital's usual time schedules and routine. Basic to the concept of patient centered care was the goal of making the patient feel more "at home" and less estranged by reducing the anxieties associated with strange situations and lack of information. Although plans included conducting a controlled study comparing the medical as well as the psychological impact of hospitalization on 3-North with that for comparable patients on other units, the patients' expression of satisfaction with the 3-North unit proved so great that many of the features of 3-North were rapidly adapted for other areas of the hospital, making an evaluation study impossible to conduct. Some of the patient satisfaction seemed due to the fact that they no longer felt trapped by hospital routine. For example, one of the special provisions of 3-North was a small serving kitchen that could provide some selected special requests (like a hamburger) and serve meals when the patients' preferred rather than on the hospital's schedule. Ninety percent of the patients on 3-North indicated that they were particularly pleased with this provision. However, only 10 percent of the patients were actually using it.

Carolyn Bacdayan who, as a research associate in behavioral science, conducted the 3-North study, provided staff work for the committee and designed the renovation of the unit, eventually became the Director of Planning for the University Hospital and in the 1980s was responsible for planning and coordinating much of the hospital's refurbishing, upgrading, expansion and systems improvements. In the 1990s, as a result of economic pressures in a highly competitive marketplace, the concept of patient centered care has achieved a substantially elevated priority nationally within the overall spectrum of health care delivery.

The 3-North project was but one episode in a continuing

process of hospital evolution that has included a complete renovation and modernization of its original floors and the construction of a major addition. It has included inservice training for new and continuing employees that focuses on consideration for the needs, fears and expectations of patients and techniques for developing sensitivity for and skills in communication with patients. New facilities include provisions for reinstating concepts that were part of the early planning. One is the helicopter service designed to speed patients in need of emergency care to the hospital while providing needed intervention en route. In 1962 a helicopter pad was built just east of the hospital providing quick access to the emergency room. Because there was no formal helicopter service, the pad received only occasional use and it was abandoned when construction of the Veterans Administration Hospital preempted its site. Although the concept was ahead of its time in the 1960s it was revived in the 1980s and with a rooftop hanger and landing pad, the aeromedical service now provides direct transportation from anywhere in the State to the hospital's emergency facilities.

Another early concept that is being resurrected is the provision for "care-by-parent" for pediatric patients. A care-by-parent unit was initially established on 4-North by Warren Wheeler, Jack Githens' successor as chairman of Pediatrics. The facility was designed to permit a parent to share a room with a child and assume much of the child's care with appropriate medical and nursing direction, thus helping to reduce the trauma of hospitalization for the child and to lower the cost of hospitalization for the family. Provisions included a washing machine, iron, snack access and a place where parents could socialize with each other. Although always considered successful, the unit was lost in a battle for space. Responding to a mandate and funding from the State legislature, the Hospital developed a substantially expanded neonatal unit. This preempted the space of a general pediatric unit that in turn preempted the space of the care-by-parent unit. In 1996, as part of the development of a Children's Hospital within University Hospital, the care-by-parent concept is to be revived and expanded.

THE PHILOSOPHY OF MEDICAL EDUCATION
AFTER FORTY YEARS

The concepts of patient centered care, care-by-parent, and even the use of helicopters to reach out to the community are all expressions of values and goals that were contained in the philosophy statement of 1956 (Chapter Four), on which much of the planning and early development of the College of Medicine was based. As discussed in Chapter Six, some of the features that characterized the College at its activation, like its innovative curriculum, were modified in a trend toward traditionalism in the 1960s. Some provisions, like the students' study areas and lounge, were lost to functions commanding a higher priority for which the planners had failed to provide. Some of the early ideas, such as the use of a helicopter, were "ahead of their time." Some, like a commitment to patient centered care, were obscured for a time by the pressure of competing priorities and traditional routines. Some, like the care-by-parent unit, were preempted in order to respond to external mandates. And some, like the "full full-time" concept for employing a clinical faculty were victims of the changing economics of health care. Yet, despite many factors of continuing change much of the Willard philosophy continued to guide the College. While more traditional than when it was originally planned and implemented, the curriculum retained some conjoint courses and a significant component in the behavioral sciences. Relationships with the rest of the University became increasingly more meaningful particularly in graduate education and research and in the participation of medical college faculty members in the University wide committee process. Bill Willard's vision that the University and the Medical Center would gain strength from each other proved prophetic and is being increasingly realized.

The College's ties to the medical profession were strengthened through the development of strong programs in continuing education. The College became a major national resource of continuing education for family practice specialists as part of their preparation for speciality board examinations. The number of clinics provided by College faculty in underserved areas increased and assistance was extended to communities seeking to increase or improve their health care resources. Outreach was not all limited to medical matters. Under the leadership of the College's fourth Dean, Robin J. Powell (Dean from 1984 to 1987), the faculty of the College of Medicine organized as "Friends of the Philharmonic" and raised funds that helped Lexington's excellent Philharmonic Orchestra survive a severe financial crisis. Powell also launched the College on to a program designed to raise funds to support the established of endowed faculty chairs.

Peter Bosomworth, who in 1970 succeeded Bill Willard as Vice President (and later became Chancellor), kept many of Willard's objectives alive although he was continually challenged by rapidly changing economic, social, political, and technological conditions. Convinced that the future of health care will require increasing collaboration among the health professionals, he was a strong advocate of the health team concept. Despite the tendency of the Medical Center's colleges each to develop independent programs, Bosomworth pushed for collaboration. He also insisted that dentistry, nursing, pharmacy and allied health be given equal voices with medicine in Medical Center wide deliberations.

One expression of Peter Bosomworth's commitment to the health team concept in medical education and service was his support for the program of Area Health Education Centers (AHEC). This program was initiated at the University of Kentucky in 1972 and initially was called the Area Health Education System. In 1974 it was expanded as a state supported cooperative effort between the Universities of Louisville and Kentucky designed to provide clinical learning experiences and services at rural sites. A basic feature of the concept was that students from several of the health professions would provide services in areas of need while learning to work together as members of a health team under the joint supervision of local practitioners and faculty members from the University. In 1975, the program qualified for federal funding. The several Area Health Education Centers, as they are now called, have been a significant component of the outreach effort of the Medical Center and its colleges for more than 20 years.

In addition to promoting the health team concept in

teaching and service, Peter Bosomworth was an advocate of greater cooperation and collaboration among various departments and disciplines in teaching and research, both with the College and Medical Center and on a University-wide basis. He presided over and encouraged the development of the concept of Centers of Excellence. Even before this concept was formally developed, a prototype was in place. Stimulated by gifts from Harlan Sanders of Kentucky Fried Chicken fame, John Y. Brown, Sr. and John Y. Brown, Jr., the Sanders-Brown Center on Aging was established in 1975 as a multidisciplinary research center concerned with the problems and diseases that are particular to the aging process. Under the direction of William R. Markesbery, a member of the College of Medicine's first class, the Sanders-Brown Center has become one of the nation's leading centers for aging research. Consistent with the initial orientation and goals of the College of Medicine, it has also assumed numerous additional functions including both professional and public education, the organization of patient and family support groups, and public information and it is the administrative home for the University's famous Donovan Scholars program that provides a variety of academic experiences for older persons.

Also extensive in its multifunctional and multidisciplinary focus is the Lucille Parker Markey Cancer Center. This had its beginning in 1979 with the Ephraim McDowell Cancer Network designed to provide statewide programs for cancer prevention, detection, diagnosis and treatment. Sparked by a gift from Mrs. Markey that was followed by several additional generous private donations, the Cancer Center is now housed in three interconnected buildings designed to provide the most modern and comprehensive approaches to treatment and research. Mrs. Markey was the widow of William M. Wright, owner of Calumet Farm, who prior to the stock market crash of 1928 had expressed his intention to give the University $10,000,000 to start a medical center (See Chapter One). In addition to her gifts to the Markey Cancer Center, Mrs. Markey established a foundation to support medical research.

Along with the Centers on Aging and Cancer, several

other Centers of Excellence have been developed in order to apply a problem focused rather than a discipline or department focused approach to research, treatment and education and to provide visibility and attract research funding for these important areas. These include Centers for Clinical Research, Alcohol and Drug Abuse, Neurological Diseases, Biomedical Engineering, Rural Health, Biotechnology and Genetic Engineering, Magnetic Resonance Imaging and Spectroscopy, and the Kentucky Heart Institute. The Centers reflect a need and a trend that was recognized during the early planning for the Medical Center when consideration was given to developing the College of Medicine without discipline oriented departments. They exemplify a concept that was ahead of its time in 1956 but is very much with the times in 1996.

By 1990, as the College was approaching the 30th anniversary of its opening, a majority of the faculty were from a new generation. They were less wedded to the Flexnerian traditions that had molded the shape of medical education for much of the 20th century and less dependent on identification with the traditional disciplines. The College's fifth Dean, Emery A. Wilson, who was appointed in 1988, unlike his predecessors, was a Kentuckian and a 1968 graduate of the University of Kentucky College of Medicine. He had returned in 1976 to a faculty position in the Department of Obstetrics and Gynecology, risen to the rank of Professor, become the founding Director of the Kentucky Center for Reproductive Medicine and spent a sabbatical leave studying management theory and techniques. If a 30 year old institution can be said to have developed traditions, Emery Wilson can be said to have been imbued with those traditions. He had entered medical school when Dr. Willard was still the Dean, the original faculty were all on hand, the unique programs in community medicine were still vibrant, and the original curriculum was still essentially in place. He had returned to the College, progressed through the academic ranks, served on key committees, and directed his own program. He was well aware of the issues, the problems, the programs and the people.

Emery Wilson brought a sense of continuity to the

College along with a strong commitment to students, patients and to the service responsibilities of the College. He set forth a statement of mission and goals that was strikingly consistent with the 1956 statement of philosophy. These are:

> To have a major role in improving the health of Kentuckians.

> To redefine medical education and educational methods through continuous curriculum improvement and educational research.

> To be recognized for significant research contributions to health and science.

> To be a courageous leader among medical schools in selected components of our mission.

> To continue our national reputation for academic innovation.

> To create an environment which stimulates optimal faculty, staff and student performance.

> To provide healthcare service and a supportive environment which exceed the expectations of our patients and their families.

> To promote integrative problem solving across disciplinary boundaries.

> To enhance economic development through research and service.

THE COLLEGE OF MEDICINE
AS A YOUNG ADULT - 1996

In 1996, the University of Kentucky College of Medicine is once again in the forefront of innovation in medical education. The College is implementing a bold new curriculum that emphasizes active student learning experiences, "problem based learning," computer based learning, small group preceptor-led instruction, the integration of some basic science and clinical learning experiences, comprehensive medicine, and the incorporation of rural and other external sites for clinical learning. The College is one of only 14 medical schools in the country to have been awarded curriculum revision planning grants and only one of eight schools to have received implementation grants for this purpose from the Robert Wood Johnson Foundation. (This put Kentucky in the company of Yale and Johns Hopkins among other recipients.)

The College, along with the University Hospital, has instituted intensive staff training and clinical program modification in order to improve the overall experience of patients being treated in the University Hospital, the emergency room and the outpatient Kentucky Clinic. The College has continued to maintain and further develop its emphasis on "patient centered care" and has extended the service for many of its out-patient programs into the evening hours.

The College has developed an extensive outreach program for both teaching and service including required student experiences in rural areas and other external clinical settings, team learning in Area Health Education Centers, residency training in family practice and other special learning experiences provided in a Center for Rural Health located in Hazard and a return to training in community medicine through a consortium of participating hospitals and private medical practices.

The College has provided leadership in the development of several University-wide, multidisciplinary Centers of Excellence.

The College's basic science departments have all developed

strong programs of research that are well supported by external funding. These departments and their programs are a major factor in the University's overall productivity in research and graduate education.

According to a recent count, the College was receiving more than 36 million dollars annually in support of its total research activity including funds from the federal government, private corporations and foundations. The College is in the top 50 percent of the nation's medical schools in terms of the research funding awarded to its faculty by the National Institutes of Health.

The College has a highly qualified medical student body represented by 95 medical students per class who have been selected from about 2,000 applicants per year.

Through its graduates and the residents it has trained, the College has contributed significantly to the current body of practicing medical professionals throughout the State.

The College is currently a community of nearly 3,500 individuals including 380 medical students, 480 residents, 150 graduate students, 570 faculty, 700 voluntary faculty, and 1,200 staff. Because of the "ripple effect" of dollars spent by the students and employees of the College, its overall economic impact on the State includes the provision, directly and indirectly, of approximately 3,300 additional jobs and a commensurate addition to the tax base, consumer spending and general economy of the State.

The College is providing medical care for the people of Kentucky through approximately 21,000 admissions annually to the University Hospital, 300,000 patient visits to the Kentucky Clinic, plus 60,000 patient visits to more than 900 clinic sessions provided by U.K. faculty in locations throughout the State.

The College is in the forefront in the development of telemedicine using modern technology to extend the benefits of the College's medical expertise in even further support of the health of Kentuckians.

The College has maintained its leadership role in applying the behavioral sciences to medical education, research and service and has received continuing recognition and support for behavioral science participation in medical education, graduate education, post doctoral training, and multidisciplinary behavioral medicine research.

჻

Just a few months after he arrived in Lexington and began the process of planning for the University of Kentucky College of Medicine, William R. Willard told a group of Rotarians "We must plan ahead for situations that are difficult to visualize and we must be flexible enough to meet these changes." Certainly these words apply as much or more today as they did 40 years ago. The rate and dimensions of change seem to grow exponentially. As these words are written the College and Medicine and medical education generally are being challenged to maintain their quality, purpose and integrity as the entire enterprise of health care faces certain though as yet undeterminable "reform" that will have an inevitable impact on the form and financing of medical education and research and on education related patient care. Hopefully, this history of the College of Medicine's early years will provide some useful perspective from the past for those who must meet the challenges of the future.

Robert Straus

ABOUT THE AUTHOR

Robert Straus came to Lexington in 1956 as a member of the planning staff for the University of Kentucky Medical Center. He served as the first Coordinator of Academic Affairs for the College of Medicine and for 28 years as Chairman of the Department of Behavioral Science in the College of Medicine (the first such department in a medical school). His honors have included election to the Institute of Medicine of the National Academy of Sciences in 1975, and a lifetime Achievement Award from the American Public Health Association in 1993. After retiring in 1987 he has remained professionally active and served for several years as part time Director for Scientific Development of the Medical Research Institute of San Francisco.

Although born in New Haven, Connecticut, Straus claims Kentucky roots for his father's family migrated to the State in the 1840's eventually settling in Louisville. Straus is a graduate of Yale University and received the Ph.D. there in Sociology in 1947. He then spent six years on the faculty of Applied Physiology at Yale specializing in alcohol studies. From 1953 to 1956 he served on the faculty of the State University of New York's Upstate Medical Center in Syracuse.

Straus is the author of more than one hundred articles and chapters dealing with behavioral aspects of health care and with problems of alcohol and other dependencies. Previous books or monographs include *Medical Care for Seamen, Drinking in College, Alcoholism and Social Stability, Alcohol and Society*, and *Escape from Custody.*

Married for more than 50 years, Straus and his wife Ruth have four children and seven grandchildren. A granddaughter, Leigh, is currently a student in the University of Kentucky College of Medicine.